"This book will lift your spirits, calm your fears, encourage your dreams, answer your questions, and confirm that you are on *your* right path! This woman of God, my dear friend, and shared presenter in the extraordinary 'God's Leading Ladies' tour gives her seasoned perspective on some of life's greatest challenges. These challenges are ones we know! She shares her personal thoughts and vast worldwide experiences, and this book will help you confirm what's possible and important for you in your 'next chapter.' As in that great quote by R.S. Grey, 'She believed she could, so she did.' You will glean advice and motivation! Most importantly, you will imagine more great things after reading these pages, and you will write your own story with verve and zest! Read this book as a gift to yourself."
—Mrs. Marian L. Heard, president/CEO, Oxen Hill Partners; retired president/CEO, Boston United Way; retired president/CEO, United Ways of New England; founding president/CEO, Points of Light Foundation

"*My Fabulous 5th Chapter* can be embraced as a post-pandemic reset guidebook, since it is crafted to feed souls, touch hearts, and enlighten our very beings. When I reached the 'Letter to My Younger Self' exercise in Chapter 5, it shook me to my core as I revisited the fear and total lack of confidence I had in my youth— and, truthfully, still experience at times. It is healing to learn that I am not alone in this journey. Therefore, my wish is for my younger sistas to heed the words and wisdom shared in this amazing book—and embrace it."
—Paula Mitchell Manning, Synergy Talent Group

"In *My Fabulous 5th Chapter*, Ambassador Dr. Sujay documents the excitement, empowerment, and endless energy of women who enthusiastically embrace the 5th chapter of their lives. In fact, the book turns on its head the traditional teaching that a woman's life after 50 is a downhill journey! Rather, women are encouraged to reimagine ordinary situations in a new season of extraordinary possibilities. Women who learn to live fabulous, faith-filled lives after 50 provide younger generations with a new paradigm for aging in the 21st century."
—Bishop Dr. Barbara E. Austin-Lucas, Agape Tabernacle International Fellowship; senior pastor/founder, Women Organizing, Mobilizing & Building, Inc. (WOMB)

"A profound and witty read on life as a seasoned woman. This book is full of wisdom from a life well lived and inspired zeal to continue living life fully. Dr. Sujay does it again, sharing biblical foundations, practical applications, and rich perspectives on living our best lives."
—Channon Lemon, catalyst for change

"Dr. Sujay's book liberated my mind and heart to experience my 5th chapter in the spirit of God's calling, with purpose and passion. There is affirmation that I am walking in the Spirit, experiencing life with no limits, and finding peace in the answer to my daily question: 'How are you going to live the rest of your life?' Selah"
—Rev. Jackie L. Williams, PhD, MA,
preacher/professor/public servant, Washington, DC

"Another fabulous read! If you are in your 'nifty fifties,' have already cruised through them, or are quickly approaching them, you MUST read *My Fabulous 5th Chapter*. I became so engrossed in this book. From personal experiences to inspiration from God and humor, Dr. Sujay is the voice and friend we yearn for as she reminds us that now is our time to shine and thrive!"
—Theresa R. Williams-Harrison, entrepreneur and *USA Today/Wall Street Journal* best-selling author; protégé/friend of Dr. Sujay

"If you're stuck in a rut or feel like you're just going along to get along, you need this book. It will fire you up and inspire you to make the rest of your life the best of your life. You'll feel like you're having a conversation with one of your best sista girls, and you'll pause, ponder, and laugh out loud. It's the book for the season of reclaiming your time."
—Pam Perry, publisher, *Speakers Magazine*

"Part memoir and part motivation, this book shows how faith, fearlessness, and stepping into God's fresh anointing is possible in any season of life. Dr. Sujay's "Litany of Self-Love" is a manifesto every woman in her 5th chapter needs to take to her heart and embrace. Bravo!"
—Joy Duckett Cain, author, *Work It! Pursue Your Passion, Live Your Purpose NOW!* Sujay's friend from childhood Sunday School, chapters 2, 3, 4, and now 5

"As one of Dr Sujay's business partners with the Global Black Women's Chamber of Commerce, I think it's great to see a book that helps us not only find our passion, but also affirm ourselves and pursue many passions, at any age and stage. Whether she's speaking or writing, or whether or not you're in the same room with her, she's a consummate professional who exudes excitement, integrity, great strength of character, grace, and pure joy and fun. I can see why she's called the 'Queen of Inspiration 4 the Nations.' I highly commend this book to you, and I plan to share it with women all over the globe."
—Brenda A. Campbell, MSW, MBA, president/CEO, USSMC, Inc.

"If 50 is the new 30, all the more reason to reflect and take stock of how we value ourselves and envision our future. We are living longer and, under the umbrella of God's will, our destiny can only be great. Dr. Sujay captures all of this, and more."
—M. Gasby Brown, MPA, CFRM,
CEO and executive consultant, The Gasby Group

"*My Fabulous 5th Chapter* is a must-read for any woman traversing her 'next' in her 50s and beyond. Through personal stories and humor, Dr. Sujay gives us an inspiring and entertaining look at how to master the inner game of reinvention with faith, flair, and fortitude. We are free to be who we are, claim what we want, and surround ourselves with those who fill us. Grab a friend (or ten) and share this book. Follow the principles and enjoy a fun, fit, and fabulous 5th chapter."

—Deb Boulanger, CEO, The Great Do-Over

"Dr. Sujay is an incredible storyteller of moments big and small. Her many talents are visible in her writing as she weaves together the brilliant threads of faith, cultural history, and family legacy. She creates a tapestry of life and offers us the opportunity to see ourselves in the storyline. In this chapter of life, she invites us all to declare, 'It's my turn.'"

—Nina Klyvert-Lawson, lifelong friend/cousin;
founder/artistic director, Project Performing Arts

"This book instills the confidence to enjoy the 50+ precious present. You'll gain insight to refocus, refuel, and refire, 'stripping off every unnecessary weight' (Hebrews 12:1) that can derail joy and a sense of peace. It will help you walk courageously into your God-given purpose in your 5th chapter."

—Lillian Moore Davenport, leadership and career strategist, End View Solutions

"OMG! My dear friend Dr. Sujay has done it again! This book tops the list of great reads that inspire, empower, and uplift. YES! This is absolutely appropriate for the lady who is determined to live her best life. The struggles of life don't stop, and for women who are 50+ and still figuring things out, this book will be a welcome friend and companion on the next leg—or, more aptly, in "the 5th chapter"—of your life. Thanks, Sujay, for the blessing of this book!"

—Dr. Teresa Hairston, author/publisher, books2liveby.com

"Affirming, inspiring, and empowering! Dr. Sujay makes clear the joys and strengths in declaring 'It's my turn now.' A must-read for every woman, even before 50!"

—Mercedes Nesfield, 88-years-young; fine, fit, and
fabulous prayer partner; retired member, NYC Board of Education

"This book is for every woman. Dr. Sujay is a true gift to us all. She is an inspirational visionary bent on transforming the world—especially women. She leads with passion and purpose in helping women who want to live their lives to the fullest. In this book of revelation, she is like a coach who has the clear road map and guides us step-by-step. *My Fabulous 5th Chapter* serves as a vital and necessary rubric to live by."

—Jennifer Vermont-Davis, chair, Community Life + Diversity team,
The Allen-Stevenson School; 3rd, 4th, and 5th chapter sister-friend of Dr. Sujay

"As we look forward to our fabulous 5th chapter, Dr. Sujay gets it right! You can feel her speaking to you, with so many relatable revelations!"

—Alexis Revis-Yeoman, lifelong friend; public information officer/legislative liaison at Prince George's County Dept. of Housing and Community Development

"A much-needed breath of fresh air for all women over 50! Dr. Sujay shares from her heart how to give ourselves permission to enjoy life to the fullest in our later years. This practical gem will open your imagination to ways of being that will make you smile and begin to live life to the fullest."

—Rev. Debora R. Barr, author/speaker, DBarr Ministries

"Enlightening and awakening, *My Fabulous 5th Chapter* is a *re-evaluative, inspiring* take on reinventing yourself with devotion, and the substance of faith, at the age of seasoned perfection. A heartfelt appreciation for what is destined, along with an inspirational, informative, and engaging display of an extraordinary meaning to the journey of this amazing gift called life."

—Carletta Burch, "The Voiceover Queen"

"Dr. Sujay inspires and guides us on fully embracing life after 50 with wisdom, health, and love. You'll be blessed by reading each chapter filled with stories about extraordinary women in her life and valuable lessons we can apply to be fabulous, free, and faith-filled during this wonderful season."

—Linda M. Stewart, contributor, *Sister to Sister: Devotions for and from African American Women;* una amiga favorita of Dr. Sujay

"Be encouraged! *My Fabulous 5th Chapter* is a guide for women who know who they are and what they want. Ambassador Sujay is reminding us all that we are worthy of every good thing from above."

—Monique J. Fortuné, EdM, MDiv, president, Fortuné & Associates; public speaking and leadership coach

"Dr. Sujay's book reminded me of how fabulous the 'nifty fifties' were for me. In fact, I have been celebrating the anniversary of being 50 for more than 15 years. Reading the stories she shares—some hilarious, and all with transparency and authenticity—I remembered how I loved who I was developing into and started loving myself all over again! As Dr. Sujay suggests, we should 'give ourselves permission' to let go of excess baggage and set our boundaries. That's why this book is so amazing. There were so many reminders and aha moments for me, and wonderful exercises to remind us of *who* we are and *whose* we are. Whether you are just entering the fabulous 50s, or beyond, *My Fabulous Fifth Chapter* helps us be sensational at every age and stage. Read this inspiring book and glide into your fabulousness with grace and ease!"

—Ms. Venita, a sensational, 60s-fabulous entrepreneur; founder/CEO, The Tyler Marcel Experience; board member, Global Black Women's Chamber of Commerce

"I initially picked up this book to peruse it, but then I couldn't put it down."

—Rev. Dr. Sheila R. McKeithen, president, Universal Foundation for Better Living

my
Fabulous
5th
chapter

IT'S MY TURN NOW!

Dr. Sujay

JUDSON PRESS
PUBLISHERS SINCE 1824

VALLEY FORGE, PA

My Fabulous 5th Chapter: It's My Turn Now!

Judson Press has made every effort to trace the ownership of all quotes. In the event of a question arising from the use of a quote, we regret any error made and will be pleased to make the necessary correction in future printings and editions of this book.

Bible quotations in this volume are from the New Revised Standard Version of the Bible, copyright © 1989 by the Division of Christian Education of the National Council of the Churches of Christ in the United States of America. Used by permission. All rights reserved. Also from *The Holy Bible*, King James Version and from The New King James Version. Copyright © 1972, 1984 by Thomas Nelson Inc.

Interior design by Wendy Ronga, Hampton Design Group.
Cover design by Danny Ellison.

Library of Congress Cataloging-in-Publication data
Names: Johnson Cook, Suzan D. (Suzan Denise), 1957- author.
Title: My fabulous fifth chapter: it's my turn now! / Suzan D. Johnson Cook.
Description: Valley Forge, PA: Judson Press, [2021]
Identifiers: LCCN 2021011249 (print) | LCCN 2021011250 (ebook)
ISBN 9780817018283 (paperback) | ISBN 9780817082314 (epub)
Subjects: LCSH: Middle-aged women. | Self-actualization (Psychology) in middle age. Classification: LCC HQ1059.4 .J63 2021 (print) | LCC HQ1059.4 (ebook) | DDC 305.244/2—dc23
LC record available at https://lccn.loc.gov/2021011249
LC ebook record available at https://lccn.loc.gov/2021011250

Printed in the U.S.A.
First printing, 2021.

To the fabulous women over fifty who are…
Ready to live this next stage of life to the fullest!!
Willing to go the extra mile with style!
Committed to being as free as you want to be,
  without guilt and apology!
Eager for relief and release!
On board to make the rest of your life the most
  blessed of your life!
Ready to decree and declare, "It's my time and
  my turn!"

Contents

Contents

Acknowledgments

I wish to thank the first women who modeled what a fabulous Fifth Chapter could look like: my mom, Dorothy C. Johnson; my grandmother, Leona Starnes Fisher Thomas; and my aunts, Martha Springs Porcher, Katherine Cyrus, and Lucille (still alive and active at ninety years old). All of these intelligent, strong women took time with me and taught me life's lessons in the pre-Spanx, pre-dishwasher, black-and-white-TV-with-a-wire-antenna, and record-player days. I watched them in every season cooking great meals, baking homemade biscuits, frying chicken, and making awesome banana pudding. I had a firsthand seat as they eased into their fifth chapters and made the ride so much fun and oh so smooth.

They all realized very early on that they had an "out of the box" young woman they were raising, yet they never "boxed me in." I was not out of control, just out of the box. I always thought differently. I wanted the "world," literally and figuratively, to travel, and to make God's and my presence known throughout the world. I knew early on that those dreams really do come true, and that dreams do not have an expiration date. If they don't come at a certain time, you don't get rid of them. Instead, you just repackage, rework, rebrand, and come back when both you and the moment are right.

Thank you for being my circle—never square. You encircled me in and with love. Thank you for always letting me soar. Thank you for being my cheerleaders and for always being at my recitals and games and acting opportunities. Even when I wasn't that great, you never let me know it. You just kept cheering me on until I got better (or realized this wasn't for me). Thank you for giving me permission to travel to Spain at the age of fourteen. Thank you for helping me give myself permission to be a wonderful woman and to help other wonderful women (and men) find their voices, make their choices, and help their voices and spirits soar. I knew life would be great for me, because you helped make it great—great for me, great for us, and great for all those who surrounded us and reminded me we serve a great God. Like I say in a prayer I wrote, we were "destined for greatness." I loved seeing you in action.

Thanks also to those who showed me how and what the Fifth Chapter could look like in your eighties, with fine-ness and finesse: my extended family; my prayer partner and travel mate, Mercedes Nesfield, a phenom; to Aunt Bertha Williams, who makes the best macaroni and cheese, and to Adele Bond, who kept up with my mother and was her running mate; and to my "amiga favorita," Lin's mom and one of my mentors, the late Melody Martin, who just left us but who lived her life to the fullest, every day and in every way. Gratitude also to the fabulous Audrey Smaltz, who could "work a runway," in front and behind the scenes, and who found and married her love in her late sixties, not online but right on time; and to our Presbyterian "moms," champions: Dr Thelma Adair and Mother Corine Cannon, who reached their 100th and 101st birthdays, and at this writing are still with and inspiring us.

I also wish to thank my "Waterside Crew," five great women who helped me to not become unglued, some of whom are in their own Fifth Chapter, living and loving life, without strife, and with whom we celebrate and share laughter and losses, love and legacy: Sully, Nettie, Delores, Turna, and Pat. Seven other remarkable women, the Washington Women of WJLA TV (the WWW Club): Lark, Thursa, Alexis, Debbie, Mary, Joy, and Pam, who have always made sure that there was food, fun, festivities, social life, and sisterhood, and who let the good times roll for almost five decades, whether on Zoom or in person.

More recently, I am blessed by the W.O.W. (Women on the Worldstage), GBWCC (Global Black Women's Chamber of Commerce), and the R.E.A.L. Women in Ministry, who are reaching, preaching, teaching, traveling, and doing everything as you are changing in your own lives and helping to be world changers, changing the lives of others, changing how the games will be played, and calling folks out who continue to "play games."

To my adult female cousins: Ingrid, Melinda, Phyllis, Jackie, Elaine, Saundra and Nina, and to my new cousins Sheryl, Dawn, Ramona, and Tanya, please keep your flow and your joy going and growing—*we* are the women warriors of our family now, and our moms are all looking down on us or right at us, and reminding us to not only make them proud but to also "party like it's 1999" (a saying in the Black culture when you really want to have fun and remember joyous eras). To my Sag Harbor, J & J, Book Club beach sisters, with whom I've shared so many dreams, defeats, and desires—from the summer circle in Sag Harbor Hills and Azurest to fundraisers, barbecues, and girls' nights out at Olivia's and Anne's, and our annual Labor Day weekend races and toasts.

To all my BFFs who have walked with me in all Five Chapters, from childhood, high school, college, my first jobs, up until now: my Sunday school classmate and childhood friend, Joy Duckett Cain to Linda, Alexis, Jennifer, and Nina (and your husbands). It's so wonderful having girlfriends in the faith, who not only prayed for me but also with me, and who I knew always had my back. Lin (and Phil), Alexis (and Felix), from having my crabs on the B'more waterfront to sharing a good steak at Del Friscos, being Godparents to our sons, sending our kids to sleepaway camp together, and enjoying sweet potato pies and turkey on Thanksgiving Day with our families. Nina (and Ron), Jen (and Stephen) for having your quiche Lorraine and the "couch" when I needed it, helping with and sowing into my campaign.

To Channon, Venita, Zelrona, and Catherine, who stayed up with me into the wee hours of the morning (when I was able to stay up or when you would wake me up), who laugh at all my dry jokes, and who help keep my soul encouraged, thanks.

And how I miss you, my dear "besties" and sisters: Yolanda King, big sister Katie Cannon, and Mom Melody, with whom I would stay on the phone for hours, sometimes all night, until the broken places were made whole and the crooked places straight, and the sun would come up on a brand-new day. You and your wisdom are still here with me in the deepest places of my heart. The world is just not the same without you, but I'm glad I had a chance to run, rock, and roll with you for almost five of life's chapters. It first felt like a "hole in my soul" when you transitioned, but now I have that "peace that passes all understanding." You're still reminding me that there is a balm in Gilead. But Venita is here, staying up to the wee hours as we laugh, party, and share our "sister secrets."

I also wish to thank the women who have journeyed with me, on all or part of it, in whichever season we found ourselves syncing in the "circle of life"—you've blessed me as much as you say I've blessed you. To all three congregations I served as senior pastor—the Mariners' Temple, Bronx Christian Fellowship (BCF), and the Lunch Hour of Power and Wonderful Wall Street Wednesday crowds. To the women at the Hampton University Ministers Conference who have cheered me on, and with whom, together, we have found our voices collectively rising (and eating fried oysters in the middle of the day or late at night—together). And to my Harlem Honeys and Bears Swim Team, all in their Fifth Chapters, thank you for inviting me to join such a great team. You have demonstrated with grace, gravitas, and grit how it should be done: synchronized swimming, at any age. You are awesome!

To Gloria, Pat, Catherine, Judge Machelle, and First Lady Trina, my "church ladies and soul sisters" who made sure my soul was anchored and my rides to and from church were secured. And to my new sisters of the global DST (Delta Sigma Theta Sorority, Inc.) family, for inviting me in and making me an honorary member, loving me unconditionally, and sharing your love and sister-hood, especially Carliss, TJ, Val, Thelma, Crystal, Venice, Zina, Sabrina, Suzanne, my Centennial Six line sisters, Sophia, and Former President 24, Cynthia Marie Antoinette Butler-McIntyre. And to one of our newest sorors, my sister-friend of three decades, who joins us in the chapter of life, CNN and American Urban Radio correspondent April Ryan, we're really so proud of you.

To Marjorie Duncan Reed, Fran Manning-Fontaine, Susan Spears, Val Harris Alleyne, Tarry Jackson, Takana Jefferson, Lois Menyweather, Joanne Meekins, Leatha Johnson, and Pat Sewell, who kept me clothed, literally and figuratively, "in my right mind," and in my right dress sizes. And to Joan Wharton and Ruth Travis, who were always the first ones to "sign up," and who helped me through my doctoral program.

Now in Chapter Five, I have some new sister friends on this part of my journey: Judy Malana, Takana Jefferson, Sabrina Dent, Paula Manning, Judy Kim, and Karen Schenk, who are helping me go to the creative places my heart has desired. To IV and Linda, for making such powerful connections and introductions, and to my boards of directors, who are helping to take me to places digitally, technologically, and multimedia-wise, into this Fifth Chapter, where I could never have gone alone.

To the Judson team, who published my very first books in Chapter Three of my life , helping my words to come alive on paper and become bestsellers, and now, in my Fifth Chapter, helping me to share this phenomenal life with others. Thanks, Linda Johnson-LeBlanc, for stopping me at the Progressive National Baptist Convention

(PNBC) and letting me share what's been on my heart and in my head and mind, and to Rebecca, Laura, Gale, Lisa, and Cheryl, for working with me. Now I'm putting it all on paper for others to be able to sing, dance, reveal, and leap with joy, as if everybody's watching. Because they are—and now, there's absolutely nothing to hide!

And last but certainly not least, this Fifth Chapter couldn't be as smooth if I didn't thank the men in my life who both celebrated and tolerated this all-the-way-live- —woman in your lively and loving ways: Ron, a great dad; Chris, my youngest, who wows me with his entrepreneurial genius and keeps me laughing; and Sam, the new Dr. Cook, our first medical doctor in the family, the loves of my life—every chapter, every day, and in every way. Thank you for being part of the *whole* journey.

Now, please go get everything life has to offer, and offer everything you can give to life. Remember to say thanks. Remember to love. You are prepared. You are ready. I'm so proud of all of you! It's *your* turn now!

A Litany of Self-Love

I Give Myself Permission...
　　To be a woman who is grateful for every day
　　　　and every chapter of my life

I Give Myself Permission...
　　To be a woman who can still be wowed and
　　　　who wows
　　To be loved
　　To forgive and to be forgiven
　　To finally be free and mean it

I Give Myself Permission...
　　To have faith
　　To eat a piece of fruit
　　To have fun
　　To look and be fine, fit, and fabulous

I Give Myself Permission...
　　To dig deep into my wells of wisdom and worthiness
　　To be sowed into but also to sow into others

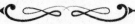

To deal with and dismiss depression
To dance like everybody's watching

I Give Myself Permission…
 To get help when I need it, and not to worry
  about who knows it
 To love, to laugh, to listen, to learn, to let go, and
  to leap for joy
 To lift up a sister when I can but to keep my own
  spirits lifted as I lift up the name of Jesus
 To turn off my electronics for the day, because
  not everyone needs to know where I am and
  what I'm doing

I Give Myself Permission…
 To listen to the birds sing, watch the streams flow,
  and watch the ocean waves dance
 To get as excited about the little things as I do
  about the big things
 To make this Fifth Chapter in my life all mine
 To proclaim it's my time and my turn, since me,
  myself, and I have arrived

I Give Myself Permission…
 To Selah—to pause, to play, pray, reflect, whenever
  I want to
 To watch sunrises and sunsets, splash in the
  waves, swim, drink flavored sparkling water,
  and sleep

To do a little or a lot of salsa, sit with a sister, or
hang out with my crew

To be confident and know that I'm all right by
myself and *with* myself

I Give Myself Permission...

To embark on my journey towards my Destiny
place, leaving behind the history people who
can't shake where they've been, and who continue
to live in the past, and who I cannot take into my
Destiny place

To not wait another minute, as the tomorrow I've
been waiting for has come *today*

To know that I have not connived to get here but have
survived to get here, and now I've arrived, I'm still
here, and so I must enjoy it

To remember that everything I want to do today I've
been planning for, praying for, and waiting for

Therefore,

I Give Myself Permission...

To finally say, "I am ready to live my *best* and
my *blessed* life—now that I have arrived at my
Chapter Five!"

Every decision you need to make, every task you need
   to accomplish,
every relationship you need to navigate, every element
   of daily life you
need to traverse, God has already perfectly matched
   up with an
equivalent-to-overflowing supply of His grace. If
   you don't agree with
that, then you either lack a proper appreciation for
   what you have,
or you are doing things that you're not supposed to
   be participating in right now.

                    —Priscilla Shirer, *Life Interrupted*

Introduction
Say Hello to Yourself

"Stop doubting your greatness and start living an awesome life."
—Jen Sincero, *You Are a Badass: How to Stop Doubting Your Greatness and Start Living an Awesome Life*[1]

Many people say that we get three chapters or three acts in life, similar to a Broadway play: Act One, Act Two, and finally Act Three—that defining moment when you're center stage in this drama-filled production called "life." On the contrary, I say we get Five Chapters. From birth through the childhood years is **Chapter One.** This is the stage where your parents are your first teachers. They celebrate the small things you do: your first step, your first birthday, and your first tooth. Most parents celebrate your first birthday as though it's your sweet sixteen, when you feel like you're the princess in your own castle.

Then, come the teenage years, **Chapter Two,** the formative years, where parents are protecting, correcting, and instructing you about life, family, and the culture you've been born into. It's a time of questioning, and you often wonder if you're doing anything right. Yet it is a fun time where your personality is formed, friends are made, sleepovers are par for the course, and curfews are given (and often broken). If you're anything like I was, my attitudes needed to be "checked" often. You spend more time looking in the mirror as your physical body begins to get its curves and swerves, and you're learning how to use it, dress it, style it, hopefully not abuse it, and gender-identify it.

As you mature into **Chapter Three,** you're entering the young-adult years. High school is wrapping up, and you begin to understand what transition is all about. Words like commencement at your graduation have real meaning because you're about to embark on a journey and go places you've never been, meeting people from all walks of life and cultures who you've never had a chance to encounter. You're learning about selections, corrections, and the choices you can make—driving, dating, drinking, sexuality and sex, college, military, or working—but you still have your parent's or guardian's wisdom and guidance (or as much of it as you can stand). The seeds they planted in you are now called "life lessons," and you are required to live *your* life. If your parents are deceased, you begin to consider how you'll manage this part of the journey without their foundation and unconditional love. If you're adopted, you might talk with yourself and others about your need to connect with your biological parents. Every time you turn on the television, ancestry.com starts running commercials until you keep feeling this "stirring" within you to know the "unknown." But whatever your situation and relationship to your family of origin, there's a gnawing of some kind at this stage of young adulthood.

You desperately want to break free from your parents but are still in their pockets, on their curfews, and must still get permission to do certain things. You start seeking wisdom, approval, and credit from other sources. Now you have more voices offering their two cents than you can handle, so you must prioritize, remain calm, or act "wild," if you're willing to suffer the consequences. If you go away to college, you might realize that you have "feelings" for someone and, although your mom or dad is not in your dorm room, their voices are still very much in your head. You feel like a rocket, about to take off and explode, but not always sure where your landing pad is located. Yet you try going into many orbits, and your choices determine how much responsibility you may have or if folks see you as being from "another planet."

Then before you know it, you're in **Chapter Four,** your adult years. You no longer have to seek parental permission to do anything. You're ready for *your* turn and to live your most blessed and best years. FINALLY!! Perhaps you've moved into your first apartment, condo, co-op, or home. Perhaps you received a college degree or spent some time in the military. Maybe you get married and maybe have kids, or you decide that you're satisfied with your single life and don't want marriage or children right now or ever. You may have saved and invested money, or you're in debt. You're clear on your socioeconomic path and determined to stay where you are, or get another degree, or work for someone else, or start a business to get further ahead. You may be focused on paying back student loans and establishing your credit.

During this chapter, it seems that in your thirties and forties you feel comfortable in your own skin, and as the fifties near, you start thinking more about facing your mortality. Insurance and financial brokers start sharing sobering news that you're closing in on the halfway mark of midlife, and you must make choices not just for you, but for your future. You need to take a serious look at life insurance, your long-term health, and your lifestyle in the event your physical and financial situation changes. This is the time to decide what and if you want to leave to the loved ones in your life and how. Political appointments, involvement, or a run for elected office may happen during this chapter. You may remodel, rebrand, rethink, reimagine, refocus, relocate, restart, and remove some people or things from your life. You may reduce some things and reprioritize.

The COVID-19 pandemic really brought a lot of this to light. Not only were more women thinking about reinventing themselves, but we saw a record number of women start new businesses.

Of course, you may find that you don't want to start anything new or restart. You're sick and tired of starting over again. You don't want to pack or unpack another box, stand in a line, move forward without a plan, or for some, without a spouse or significant other. In fact, you start reprioritizing rather than repacking. You try to decide what you can throw away or give away, and from whom you can tear away, steal away, leave, or purge. For many, particularly as their forties and fifties end, they start decluttering, de-stressing and de-toxing from anything or everything that affects their rhythms of life. I have found many in this Chapter Four, who attend my retreats, usually so busy from running themselves ragged that they declare "there's got to be a better way." So really what I end up doing is forging adult "play dates."

You decide how much scrutiny you want to live under, if any, and how much anonymity. You realize that technology is here to stay and make a decision if it will be your friend or your foe. You may work for a campaign or against one or sit in front of the news broadcasts for hours hearing others' viewpoints on a hot topic. You may contribute to the conversation every now and then—on your own terms, in your own timing. You've sat under and with the teachings of many, so you are well-rounded. You put dates on your calendar that are truly important to you. You've got real choices. If you're in good health, or even if you're not, you can choose to change the direction of your life. At the very least, you can make a list of the dreams you still have—your "bucket list."

Chapter Four is often the sandwich-generation stage, which means you may have children to still care for as well as aging parents. Even though your energy has been good, you didn't ask for this. You may have overcome a recent illness, received a diagnosis, or determined that you need more self-care. Sadly, you may have lost friends who were about your age, and you realize that, as the soap opera says, you do only have *One Life to Live*. It's not time to *Search for Tomorrow* but to seize today. *You* decide what that means for you. And you often begin to face your own mortality.

Whether married or single, gay or straight, hooked up or looking for a hookup, or don't care, you are making decisions about who you want in your life at this stage of your journey. You're deciding who your he-roes and she-roes are, whether you want or need a life coach, and if you have the energy, health, or resources to do the things you've dreamed of doing. Of course, you may still have some debt, whether it consists of student loans, car loans, mortgages, or loans from (or to) a relative, yet you are more disciplined and have a better handle on your finances. Or, from a personal standpoint, you may have some baggage that you're really ready to deal with or shed. From a career standpoint, you can actually begin to see retirement. You may realize that you made some good decisions and some bad ones, and perhaps you are not sure if and how to get out of the latter. This is a moment when you decide whether you'll accept the status quo, not deal with it, or have just enough energy to challenge it once again. In many respects, you have started to establish a routine, some say a "rut-ine," and you're just not satisfied getting a cup of coffee at 7 a.m., eating a bagel at 8 a.m., and then vegetating on the game shows, followed by the news shows, followed by the nightly features. You know which shows are on when, and whether or not you identify with the story lines. So, *this* is how my Fifth Chapter is going to be?

> "*At age 20, we worry about what others think of us.*
> *At age 40, we don't care what they think.*
> *At age 60, we discover they haven't been thinking of us at all.*"
> —Anonymous[2]

Say Hello to Yourself

Drumroll, please! You have arrived at your defining moment. Lights, camera, action, red carpet! Here we are together in our **Fifth Chapter**. I'm not just researching and writing about it—I'm *living* it. This is real life. I'm either "on the job, out of a job, no longer on the job, retired from a job, but not a lot of startups." You're just praying you can still "get up." **It's the chapter *after* your fiftieth birthday, and all the way until the end of life.** Most of us don't even put candles on our cakes—if we have a cake at all. Some of us have to watch our sugar intake, so it may just be small slice of pie, not a whole piece. This is when you really say hello to yourself, your real authentic self, and say goodbye to all the phonies, fakes, facsimiles, and fibbers. It's truly *fabulous!* You are free. You don't have to pretend. Your AARP card arrives, like clockwork, on the big 5-0 birthday, and its sobering. You don't have anything else to prove even though you never did but thought you did. It's all yours! It's what I call "making a 'you' turn."

Making a "You Turn"

Before, the world pressured you; now, allow it to pleasure you. Before, there were few options; now, you can create new options beyond receiving your AARP card in the mail. Your perspective is different, not difficult. Your assurance is fortified. You are confident, not arrogant. You can feel "a new thing" about to happen, perhaps just as Isaiah did, when he prophesied; ... can't you see it?" (Isaiah 43:19).

You can create new opportunities. Before, you said "hello, world" and hoped that others would respond and accept you, not reject you or ignore you. Yet now, you can say with confidence, "Hello self! With whom do I have the pleasure of speaking?" It's really rhetorical. You don't need a reply from anyone else. You ask and answer your own fabulous questions and do not allow others to interpret, intercept, interrupt, interrogate, intimidate, imitate, investigate, or overwhelm you. They may give you their opinions, and you can be bold enough to say, whether to yourself or to them, "I wasn't really asking your opinion."

When I was going through the long, drawn-out White House vetting process and Senate confirmation hearings for my post as U.S. ambassador-at-large, many had opinions about what I should or should not allow myself to do, and whether I should hold on or fold in. Many would always start with, "If I were you. . ." I remember saying to myself, and one day out loud, "But you are *not* me, and I don't remember them asking *you* to go through the hearings." I wasn't being rude. I was just establishing my boundaries, building my confidence, and knowing who and whose I was. It was also a moment of having real clarity for what I was willing to tolerate as it pertained to or about *me*.

This is *your* Chapter Five, when you suddenly realize it's all right to talk to yourself—and come up with your own fabulous answers! This isn't the Hollywood TV show *Jeopardy,* where everything hinges on your final question and answer. This is *your* reality show, where you create the categories, realities, and narratives for your own life: fine, fit, and fabulous!

Chapter Five also ignites love emotions at this age, at any time of day, married or single. If you're married, it takes some renegotiating with your spouse, requesting new attentiveness, or sometimes requesting more space. You both redefine what being a couple means for you, and you read or re-read *The 5 Love Languages*.[3]

If you're single—whether widowed or divorced—it's very interesting to be in the dating scene once again. Whatever decade you're in, one thing is for certain: you can't relive your past, but you can create a great "right now." You've grown; you have new needs; you're forming new perspectives. I like to say we're seasoned, but not sagging. If you're single or single again, you may glance at a handsome man, or search dating websites for the one who seems "right" for you. There may be a real desire inside you that's been waiting and raring to go or to come out. Dating sites or exclusive dating services may be on your favorite lists, and you find yourself picking up a copy of one of "Dr. Ruth's books referring to sex or Shmuley Boteach's book *Kosher Sex: A Recipe for Passion and Intimacy*, or Christian books about sexuality, because Christians sometimes don't have honest conversations about sexuality, not at any stage or age, but especially for their "seasoned saints." You may find yourself wrestling with your faith and your hormones. But sometimes you'd just like a companion to share with, to hold, to laugh and love over a meal while honoring your vow to single celibacy.

Your faith is also a revelation in Chapter Five. You have a long-standing relationship with God, and no one church building, or worship experience defines or limits your faith. Didn't we experience this during COVID-19? Most were not able to enter buildings, so relationships became more of a priority. You take the training wheels off. You've had a lifetime on this ride. Especially now, in this virtual age, you can now decide if the services at your current church are meeting your needs, are too long, too stuffy, too rigid, too conservative, too narrow, or just no longer relevant or inspirational enough for you. Maybe it's no longer a good fit for you. You redefine what having a "church home" really means. Or maybe you've become so comfortable in your pajamas during the pandemic that using Zoom is a better fit for you. It's up to you to determine what you need, if, how, when, and how often you need it, and which, if any, ministries you will be involved with.

Another Chapter Five reminder happens when you ride on public transportation and the men now jump up and say, "Ma'am, would you like to sit down?" You don't want to admit it, but you really wanted to sit down and were praying someone would get up and offer you a seat. But the fact that they probably did so because of your age just messes with your head.

Now you enjoy certain freedoms, such as the freedom to choose what you wear, how you wear it, or if you'll develop your own style, without a stylist. The freedom is that you've paid your life dues, and the choice is yours to show up cute, seasoned, sassy, or salty. Didn't Jesus say, "You are the salt of the earth; but if salt has lost its taste, how can its saltiness be restored?" (Matthew 5:13). Stay salty, my sister. You've got savor and flavor.

Turning fifty doesn't mean you have to have a midlife crisis. It is the beginning of the rest of your life. Your best and most blessed days are yet to come, and you can reinvent, reimagine, rebrand, reduce, remove, retire, or even relocate. You can begin to alter your rules, live honorably but without so many restrictions. I slept until noon one day recently, at first felt guilty, and then freed myself up. There was nothing to do that day, no schedule, no agenda. My body needed the uninterrupted restful sleep, and I felt like a million dollars for the rest of the day. I had to change the rules that had been in my head for three generations. My mother had awakened us on Saturday mornings, as her mother had awakened her, to do chores and work on the family farm. But no longer are my kids around. I can clean my house on any given day at any given time (or hire someone).

You're not marching to anyone else's drumbeat now. You can have whatever you want for breakfast, brunch, lunch, or dinner. Maybe you're a circle that's been trying to fit into a square all this time, and you just found out that you can draw another circle, and this one's even better. Chapter Five is when you and God develop a deeper love and affection for one another, and the meaning of life is not sought after anymore. Instead, now your dance with the Creator is synchronized, and you begin to reflect on your life and whether it had been well lived. Some call it your legacy. It's asking yourself the questions "How did I do?" and "How am I doing?" You try to move as one (at least most of the time) with God. Revelations are stronger, and you begin to understand Acts 17:28: "In him we live and move and have our being." But sometimes the "moving" part gets out of whack, and you find the parts that moved when you went to bed suddenly go on strike the next morning, and refuse to move.

If truth be told, you can't run or hide from the numbers that follow your fiftieth year. Nevertheless, it's never too late to find new meaning, new insight, new significance, or new ways to express your age and create the life you want for this season. The main point I want to stress is that you must really give yourself permission and "just do it!" (as Nike reminds us). Regardless of when and where you picked up this book, this read is just for you. It does not matter what you have not done up to this point. What matters most is that you are ready to soar, to receive all that life has to offer. It's *your* time and *your* turn to live out this Fifth Chapter and make it the best chapter ever! Make it Fabulous!

CHAPTER ONE

Is Your Fifty Nifty?

"Today is the oldest you've ever been, and the youngest you'll ever be again."
—Eleanor Roosevelt[4]

I like to say that your fifties can be nifty, but they can also be "shifty." All kinds of things are happening to you, with you, around you. And we must learn how to respond to them with a mature approach. We have lived five-plus decades. We are mind, body, and spirit. And our needs change with time. The body is definitely shifting, and one's mental and physical health are critical at every stage of life, but especially at this major milestone. At this writing, our nation is going through a crisis. A pandemic can cause one to panic, and different ages and stages in life can cause you to react in various ways. For me, turning fifty, losing a dear friend, and being appointed to a global White House office, all compounded together, afforded me a range of emotions. In this chapter I will be sharing some true-life stories and how they have impacted me, both positively and negatively.

How we respond to our circumstances has a lot to do with how we go forward. Two of the things that were helpful to me in my fifties, which I commend to you:

1. Limit the amount of news you receive and the time you receive it. The only time I watch the news is right before I go to dinner. I refuse to watch the news just before I go to bed. The last thoughts of my days I try to keep positive, and not allow my subconscious to wrestle with negative thoughts and images all night long.

2. The other thing I do (and did throughout all my decades) is find uplifting reading material that shares stories of people who are where I want to be at my stage of life. I hope this book helps you with your life as it is right now.

Many books have inspired me, and the conversations and interviews with those in their Fifth Chapters have been meaningful, revealing, reviewing, insightful, and delightful. Some have horror stories, others are less tragic, and some are almost magic. I'm able to reflect on the good things that happened, now that I'm in my sixties, I also realize that some who are about to enter Chapter Five may not feel nifty. I say, "Hold on! You're getting there—and it is closer than you think." I like to liken it to driving. When you start out in the dark, you have only thirty feet of light from your headlights, but you don't stop driving because you know that as you go, more light will come to you, and you will get through and to your destination. In life, this is the maturing stage. We've been on a few rides and had a few drives in our lives. And we know that there is light, not just at the end of the proverbial tunnel, but in and out of all the tunnels and funnels of life. So, we've stayed on the road, had a few accidents along the way, taken a few wrong turns—and Lord knows we've had some detours, hit some potholes, been stuck in traffic, and had to make some "you turns," but we've made it to our Fifth Chapter. I encourage you throughout this book, to make a "you turn" and put some markers on those significant moments.

A significant milestone for me was my actual fiftieth birthday. The day started out with a bang! Quite nifty, I had two events over the course of two days. First was my Lunch Hour worship service, Wonderful Wall Street Wednesday, where President Clinton, whom I had served when he was president, came to celebrate with me and was the keynote speaker. My best friend, the late Yolanda King, the eldest daughter of Martin Luther King Jr. also came. Then, the very next day, we had a huge party, with Sen. Chuck Schumer (now Senate Majority Leader), Rev. James Forbes, Bishop Dennis Proctor, and Rev. Al Sharpton among the guests, along with a host of my favorite family and friends. I wanted a real party, with music, dancing, festivities, and we had one!

But then shortly thereafter both my brother, Charles, and Yolanda died.

So my fiftieth year was filled with highs and lows, triggering me to feel like I was ready to leave where I was but didn't know how. I had a hole in my soul, and I also felt like climbing into a hole. Grieving is extremely hard for public figures because, although one's life may be public, grief is also very private and touches you in the raw, very personal places of your heart and soul.

Since I birthed children in my late thirties, when I hit my fifties, I had a lot on my plate, and some of it was not so nifty. It was nifty that my sons were becoming independent young men, both in high school and one starting to apply to colleges. But I still had to make a living, and we were in that middle income bracket, so scholarships were limited. Not so nifty.

I was feeling a restlessness in my spirit about staying where I was. Because of their ages, I knew I had certain freedoms I hadn't had before. They could now take public transportation back and forth to school, to games ,and to social events. But I was raising two African American sons in inner-city New York, so I was always conscious of how much time I would be away at work. I believe the mother is the first teacher, and parental presence is very important in children's lives.

At the same time, my energy for pastoral ministry was waning. One definition of *waning* is that the light begins to diminish. My stress level was going up while my flame was going out. My candle had no more wick. In fact, my youngest son asked one day, "Mom, didn't you write a book *Too Blessed to be Stressed?* When I answered yes, he said, "Mom, it's time to read your own book." Wow!

I'm not sure when or where I discovered it, but somehow and somewhere Barbara Brown Taylor's book *Leaving Church: A Memoir of Faith* was commended to me. I read it cover to cover. In it, she's extremely transparent, disclosing how, after a three-decade-long parish ministry career, she was feeling what she described as "compassion fatigue." I felt that was the exact place I was in life and in ministry. She describes how she finally permitted herself to "have a life." I saw so many parallels in our two lives: we had been ordained around the same time, and served about the same amount of time, just in different faith traditions. What I remember most is her describing how, at her retirement party, she jumped into the swimming pool with her clothes on and how liberating that was! As one who loves swimming, I could relate not only to the analogy but also to what it must have felt like. Had it been a movie, I could picture that scene and would have been glued to my seat—and not even thinking about getting popcorn.

This was right around the time I was burning out from a three-decade-long senior pastorate in inner-city New York. Having served as a senior pastor in the Baptist church during my Chapters Three and Four, by the time I was embarking and starting into Chapter Five, I was burnt out, but felt obligated to my "calling" (due largely to my never let them see you sweat, never give up, up-bringing). Yet I knew I could not plan another retreat, another women's day celebration, another youth day or excursion, not even another Bible study. (Remember, this was pre-digital age, we didn't have Zoom, so every idea had to be implemented in person.) It was time. I was in my fifties. It was supposed to be nifty, but I was about to crash. I needed something to shift.

I had been raised by parents who lived through the Great Depression and wanted to make sure that we always had everything we needed because they had had very little. So, my Chapters One, Two, and the beginning of Three were greatly impacted by my culture and context. They were my parents. Loving, yes, but they had a drive that was motivated by never wanting to go back into poverty. For me, failure was not an option. Quitting was not an option. For many, Saturdays were rest days, but for us, it was "get up and do your chores" days. As a result, I've been driven, going fast and hard every day for most of my life. I performed most tasks with ease, so people always thought I was pretty smooth and fulfilled. But by age fifty, I was tired and worn out. *Leaving Church* gave me permission to give *myself* permission to shift gears. The light bulb came on. It was no longer about having to prove the "calling." I was literally "falling" apart.

I had been true to what God had asked/assigned me to do—for three decades. But now, my season was changing. I needed God to do a "new thing" with me and in me (see Isaiah 43:19). I needed my fifties to be nifty.

Barbara's book helped me identify what I was feeling: "compassion fatigue." I was exhausted from doing the pastoral care I'd been giving for thirty years. I needed a change. I needed to make some moves. Sometimes you make the moves, and sometimes the moves come to you. It's believing what the Holy Scriptures declare that God will give you the "desires of your heart" (Psalm 37:4). The world may call it making your "bucket list." People of faith say, "Go for it!"

When my son was admitted to the college of his choice, and after I read Barbara's book, the yes-es were lining up for me to be courageous and admit that life has its stages, and I was embarking on the next one. It was relief and release. God was using Barbara to speak to me.

Barbara's was the voice I had been waiting for but didn't know it. She allowed my inner voice to be amplified. I was not leaving the "call of God." I was still on God's team, but ready to change uniforms—oh my, it was so liberating! We see it all the time with sports. I used to live near Yankee Stadium, and we sometimes "fall in love" with baseball stars, especially pitchers. Well, the next season we return to the stadium, and the star pitcher we knew from last season may be gone from the Bronx, but he did not leave baseball. He just signed with another team and changed uniforms. The thing about freedom and going forward is that you don't always know where, but you do know *when*—when your season is changing, when you are ready to have that metamorphosis, to change from a caterpillar into a butterfly. I could feel my wings.

More freedom and confirmation came next from Susan Crandell's book *Thinking about Tomorrow: Reinventing Yourself at Midlife*. Susan profiled men and women who had longed to do certain things but who didn't because of career obligations, and the need to "make a living." Now they were ready to "have a life." For example, there was a corporate bank executive who had always wanted to own a zoo. Well, he retired and opened one. Another woman had wanted to ride in a hot air balloon, and she finally did it. Susan herself went from a lucrative career as a magazine publisher and editor, to writing books about all the things she and others wanted to do with their lives. The stories in Susan's book were not only liberating, but also ignited something within me to make my next move on my terms. I knew I was ready for my next step, but I didn't feel like it was early retirement.

About this same time as I was reading these inspiring books, I received a phone call from the State Department. It was Hillary Clinton's office. A position for a U.S.

Ambassador for International Religious Freedom was becoming available, and my name had been brought up to be considered as a candidate. I would be nominated by Secretary Clinton and appointed by the first African American president of the United States, Barack Obama. Would I be interested?

Can I spell YES in all caps? I've learned that the only place for lamentations is in the Holy Bible. We don't need to go around lamenting but rather being thankful to God "in all circumstances" (1 Thessalonians 5:18). The apostle Paul said, "I have learned, in whatever state I am, to be content" (Philippians 4:11).

This was my second run at the White House. This time I stayed four years, part of my Fifth Chapter, from ages fifty-four to fifty-eight. Soon after I finished my tenure with the White House and State Department, I had dinner with a friend who was about to turn sixty. In addition to planning a fabulous sixtieth birthday party, she established a new professional presence. Like me, she was ready for a new move. She was ready to plan for retirement but wanted to work at least another decade. As part of her plan, she would eventually move to her hometown to be with the people she loved and in the places that make her happy.

After meeting with this friend, I started making a new bucket list, and so many things came bubbling out of me. Although I had done a number of unconventional things in life, I felt restricted because of traditions, fears, and family. I can't tell you what a relief it was to lay all that aside and release the creative juices that were feeling like volcanic lava inside of me, about to explode and pour over into the sea of my soul. At that moment, I realized, yes, there is much life in the fifties, not just for those to whom I ministered, but also for me!

I wanted what Jesus wanted for me: to "have life, and . . . have it more abundantly" (John 10:10). Abundant joy, abundant finances, abundant family time, abundant travel, abundant movie night outings, abundant bid whist games, abundant Friday and Saturday night hangouts without having to prepare a Sunday morning sermon, abundant walks without having two cell phones and a beeper on at all times, abundant joy at the beach house. My abundant list goes on and on, and so can yours. Do you hear me, my Fifth Chapter sisters? Am I making myself clear enough? I hope so. The Fifth Chapter means all the years past fifty. It's any day after your fiftieth birthday, and carries us into our sixties and as long as "you shall live." You're with and in this chapter until "death do us part." So, while you're alive, LIVE!!

Some of my Turning Points
"Here's what I know: I'm a better person at fifty than I was at forty-eight . . . and better at fifty-two than I was at fifty. I'm calmer, easier to live with." —Patti LaBelle[5]

Halftime
For some, change may begin in the late forties, but there's something about age fifty that's noticeably different: physically, emotionally, mentally, spiritually. It's when we have reached our hypothetical halfway mark, somewhat like sports. Halftime signifies a shift in the atmosphere. It's a stoppage of the game and a shutdown of sorts. Both

teams take locker room breaks, receive their notes and lessons from the coach, run over plays, while spectators run to the restroom and grab a bite to eat. It's a time to stretch and mingle. If you were cold the first half, you pull out your blanket. If you were hungry, you stand in line for your hot dog. If it's the Super Bowl on TV, you stay and watch the halftime show.

Happy Fiftieth Birthday

Similarly, at age fifty, things begin to shift, and new choices are made. You, too, take a break; it may not be in a locker room, but you are more methodical and strategic about vacations, naps, visiting. You, too, run over the plays of your first half. We call it "reflection," and you stop long enough to get lessons from the coach. You look back at the first half and start to think about how and what you can do differently, whether personally or professionally. Your body and surroundings will let you know. For one thing, our physical bodies may begin to do things—like contort, cave in, expand, wrinkle, sag, sink, cramp, or just make you cringe when you look in the mirror. What happened to our beautiful temple of the Holy Spirit?

The reminders of this magnificent milestone start to show up all around us. Without warning, an AARP card arrives in your mailbox, on your fiftieth birthday, addressed to you with all your titles, names, middle initials, and surnames, correctly spelled, welcoming you to your new season. It makes you face reality so that life does not throw you a curve ball. I recall my initial "hysteria" upon the receipt of that AARP card. It was not a pretty moment, as I couldn't believe how I hit the age fifty mark at what felt like warp speed.

Another Turning Point

Three other major occurrences were turning points that nudged me into accepting my new chapter. The first was just around my fiftieth birthday. I was drawn to Bob Buford's book *Halftime: Moving from Success to Significance*, which is about Christian men in the middle of their lives. Having been an athletic female and having chosen a profession that was dominated by men, I often found myself in the room with a lot of them. The libraries and venues that hosted many of these events were themselves often masculine in décor, filled with male "stuff," like magazines for men, hunting gear, and certainly football gear, memorabilia, and literature. I was raised with a lot of strong men in my family and surroundings, dads, uncles, cousins, neighbors. I am usually quite comfortable in a so-called "man's world" and have always been drawn towards success principles. So, the title of Buford's book, *Halftime*, caught my eye and my interest.

As I read it, I was overjoyed with the energy and the analogies, but then I realized that all of the illustrations were comparisons with *men* on the playing field in the second half of their lives. Now remember, I'm a pre-Title IX sports woman, when women didn't get the sports scholarships nor training—and anyone fifty-five and over can relate. We didn't have the attention to women's sports as did men—so it was obvious in these settings that they were referring to men. None of the analogies or great metaphors were intended for me. I just put in the back of my mind that one day I, too, would write a book, and it would be for women, not bent over on the fifty-yard line of a football field, but whose lives had major transition points: marriage, kids, kids off to college, death of parents and siblings and friends, and the empty-nester syndrome. Yes, we may have to make some tackles and get well-deserved touchdowns, but we also have to tend to some other "women only" things that occur in our lives, particularly physically.

It was interesting because the more and more I read the "halftime books for, by and about men, the more I noticed they were looking to do something "good in the community, or elsewhere, as many of them had been corporate and focused on their careers, whereas many women after fifty are finding their voices and making some choices. Depending on where and how they were raised, many put careers on hold, and they took care of their families, and did the "community" things prior to age fifty.

Now or Never

Another turning point was born out of tragedy. Shortly after my fiftieth birthday celebration, Yolanda King, my best friend, who had been with me for the two-day celebration, and most of the celebrations we'd shared since college, suddenly passed away. Not only had Yolanda and I had the "best time ever" hanging out at the fiftieth birthday party and afterwards, but that year we'd spent more time together than ever before. We had vacationed together. We both were public speakers, but were usually in different cities at different times, on different days. That year, however, we had been on the same stage speaking and had frequently stayed in the same hotel in the months leading up to my birthday. Yolanda had been with me the entire week and at all of my parties and celebrations. We had partied, played, and prayed together. The night of my birthday party, we were in my hotel suite stuffing our faces with tortilla chips and all kinds of dip, giggling about how we were going to lose weight soon. We had even selected my birthday celebration based on the dates that she could come to New York to help me celebrate, even though it was actually three months after the actual date.

To say I wasn't ready for her death is a vast understatement. I crashed emotionally, fell apart. She was not only my best friend but also the godmother of my youngest son, whose birthday she was shopping for just days before she left us. God, how could this be? Giggling one minute, and sobbing hysterically the next?

Yolanda was ready to really live it up in her Fifth Chapter. She had told me that she had in the past put her personal dreams on hold to take care of family business on the East Coast, but had just made up her mind to move back West to pursue her real dream of acting in Hollywood. Unfortunately, my dear friend never was able to realize that dream. Shortly after she landed in Los Angeles, she suddenly dropped dead at the age of fifty-one, just as she was beginning her Fifth Chapter.

Needless to say, I was ripped apart to lose my friend, but her death also brought home the realities of life, at any age, and especially after fifty. Mortality became real in a way that was life-changing and a rude awakening. I thought to myself, *If I don't do some of the things I've been wanting to do now, then when? I might never have the chance again.* This was my wake-up call, and it should be yours as well. We give so much of ourselves to everyone else. Now it's time to give yourself permission to do some of the things you'd like to do.

The Rude Awakening: Another Turning Point As I Hit the Next Decade, Age Sixty

I thought the fifties were something but the thing about the Fifth Chapter is that it is filled with surprises. Most of the people who could have told and prepared you for what it's really like, are usually gone, by the time you get there, and you suddenly stop looking for the "matriarch of your family" and become one. So for me, the fifties were nifty, and the sixties were seasoned and savory, full of new flavors. I often told folks that I was like a Paella, Paella is a flavorful dish in the Latinx culture, especially from Spain. I am a P-Pastor-A-Author-E-Entrepreneur-LL-Leading Lady and A-Amazing Diplomat.

> **P** = Pastor
> **A** = Author
> **E** = Entrepreneur
> **L** = Leader
> **L** = Lady
> **A** = Amazing Diplomat

The years and seasons seemed to fly by. It seemed like one week you're in your fifties and you look up, and boom—you're really a boomer and now in your sixties.

So when the week before my sixty-second birthday hit, I was walking into my favorite pool site, run by the New York City Parks Department. I was "feeling good in my neighborhood." In my mind, I was two decades behind my actual age. But everything else pointed to "Now you are a senior citizen, claim it."

I had just enough time to swim for forty-five minutes, but it was also renewal time for my ID card. I needed to get out in a hurry for my next appointment, but I just couldn't pass up my morning swim. I asked the attendant to please run the credit card for my payment while I was in the water and have my receipt ready when I returned. But my renewed identification card was not ready. When I asked why, I was told that my old membership was *not* at the senior rate, and with my sixty-second birthday being two weeks away, wouldn't it make more sense for me to wait the two weeks to get the discounted senior rate? How sobering, to say the least. "Oh no! Not me!" I exclaimed. When did this happen? Yes, it was a great deal economically, but it took the wind out of my sails. I wasn't ready to be a "senior citizen" yet.

I kept thinking, *When did the years go by? Where did they go? Was I in a place where I, like the Scriptures and Paul, could say, "I've learned to be content in whatever state I'm in," or was I simply frozen in my own fears of aging?* Did anyone notice that I was kicking and screaming my way further into my Chapter Five? The handwriting was on the wall. In two weeks I would officially be a *senior citizen.* Not only could I receive the senior discount rate at most venues, but folks now offer me their seat on the New York City subway. Maybe I needed to shift my perspective. Perhaps I had *earned* the right to sit on the subway after all these years.

The most recent turning point was when my firstborn son graduated from medical school. I helped him financially during this last year because of the high cost and high pressure on medical students. My son and I talked regularly to make sure things were straight and all of his deadlines were met. But his graduation meant those frequent conversations would soon be over. He would begin his Residency. He would have plans: morning plans, work plans, evening plans, and life events without me. For his graduation, it was a privilege to take him, along with his brother (who was celebrating his twenty-fourth birthday on the same day) and his girlfriend, and their dad out to dinner at McCormick and Schmick's Seafood Restaurant. Everyone ordered whatever they wanted. There were no rations, nor did we have to share an entrée. We had a great time. We laughed, hugged, cried, took pictures, made champagne toasts, and wished him well.

After dinner, the young adults went out to party while the parents got back on the train from Philly to DC. My sons' rooms were neat, with beds made up. This was the first time in a long time that I was in the house with neither sons nor spouse. No one was depending on me. No one expected accountability from me. I was finally "free"—from tuition payments, soccer practices, baseball games, and pick-ups from late-night events. I was free to not cook dinner or eat a wholesome meal. I could have cornflakes for dinner, or steak for breakfast—this is the life! I stood frozen in my kitchen and thought to myself, *I'm in my Fifth Chapter, and it really is my time and my turn. Now that it's here, what on earth will I do with it?*

It's now or never. Everyone has a date of birth on their birth certificate. And sooner or later, there will be a date of death on your death certificate. On the program for your funeral or homegoing or celebration of life service or memorial service, your "sunrise" year will be recorded, along with the date of your "sunset." In between, there's a dash. That dash represents your entire life: what you did with your life, whether you enjoyed it or complained about it, whether you left a mess or a legacy. Since you are reading this book, there is no death certificate yet, so you can do something with your dash. The choice is yours. You are the queen of your own life and God-designed destiny. The Bible says we are "joint heirs" to the throne (see Romans 8:17). I encourage your Royal Highnesses to walk through this Fifth Chapter with ease. Now that you've been educated, motivated, and invigorated, it's finally time to be liberated!

KEEP IT MOVING!!

No matter what your physical, emotional, mental, or spiritual state, you need to keep your body moving. One of the most important ways to feel nifty is to move: walk, run, bike, stretch. Find something you can do daily, and even more than once a day if you're able. But please do something. Whether on foot or in a wheelchair, the mobility of the limbs and muscles you are able to move is critical. I just talked on the phone with a girlfriend who has had several surgeries this year. After a while she said, "I have to hang up now because I'm going to do some wheelchair walking alongside my daughter as she takes her walk." She said that "my medicines can make me sleepy, irritable, and not wanting to move. But I need the exercise and the fresh air."

During the COVID-19 pandemic, I found a safe place to exercise and see the beauty of God's earth—the beach parking lot near where I live. I can do my devotions (I call myself a "Bayside Baptist" rather than a "Bedside Baptist), I can walk around the parking lot (three times is a mile), and I can get outside in God's fresh air. One day I saw a family of ducks in the water, swimming in formation behind the matriarch, and I just stopped to watch and enjoy. I thank God for sight, smell, sound, taste, and breath. "Praise him in his mighty firmament.... Let everything that has breath praise the LORD (Psalm 150:1b, 6a).

Your Next Move: Your Nifty Fifty Exercise
Fill the spaces below with an honest self-assessment of what you've done and where you'd like to go.

Accomplishments

Things I Wish I Had Done Better

What Will It Take to Get There?

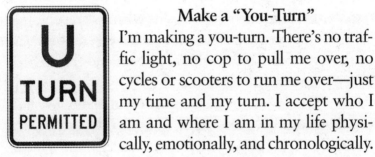

Make a "You-Turn"

I'm making a you-turn. There's no traffic light, no cop to pull me over, no cycles or scooters to run me over—just my time and my turn. I accept who I am and where I am in my life physically, emotionally, and chronologically.

CHAPTER TWO

The Word Says So

"Be patient with yourself. Self-growth is tender; it's holy ground. There's no greater investment."—Stephen R. Covey[6]

The number five has the biblical meaning of God's grace. In Hebrew, the number five refers to being saved or rescued. God is the one who saves us when we repent, turn around, and follow. The number five symbolizes "a bridge between God's realm in heaven and the physical life of [humanity]."[7]

Five is also known as the number of humanity. We have five fingers and five toes on each hand and foot. We have five major appendages (two arms, two legs, and a head), five senses (sight, sound, smell, taste, and touch), and five major body systems (circulatory, respiratory, skeleton, digestive, and nervous).

Biblically, four is the number of man/woman's weaknesses, and when you add the number one to it, you get five, which indicates God's grace! In this Fifth Chapter of your life, you can thank God for God's goodness and grace, and then it's your job to put all that goodness and grace to work. Go for it! Go for everything God intended you to have and to do. As Romans 12:2a advises us: "Do not be conformed to this world but be renewed by the transforming of your mind."

The Five Daughters of Zelophehad

Women are phenomenal. Some Orthodox Jewish men still pray, as part of an ancient model prayer, "Thank God I am not a woman."[8] Let me be clear. I'm so glad that I *am* a woman!

There are five awesome biblical women whom I'd like you to know: the daughters of Zelophehad. I am amazed at how their journey resonates with mine. They inspired my own Chapter Five. Their story is found in the Old Testament in Numbers 27:1-11. It's a fascinating story that God thought important enough to include in the biblical history.

The names of Zelophehad's daughters are Mahlah, Noah, Milcah, Tirzah, and Hoglah. Each name has significance and demonstrates their boldness not to be held back by their gender or by negative labels. All their names have both a masculine and feminine Hebrew meaning. For example, Mahlah means disease, weak, or sick, yet she stood strong with her sisters to ask for her rightful inheritance.[9] Noah, which is a gender-neutral name, means "shaky girl" or "lady wanderer" in its feminine form. In its masculine form, ark-building Noah means "rest," "repose" or "comfort."[10] Milcah stands for "queen" or "counsel," and the male meaning is usually translated as "king."[11] The name Tirzah is found twice in the Bible, as Zelophehad's daughter and as the name of a beautiful city. The Hebrew meaning is a "delight," "pleasantness," or "to be pleased with or favorable to."

Tirzah's power was in her favor, and we all know that when favor is being given it may not be equally distributed[12] Finally, Hoglah means "partridge" or "to wobble or hop."[13] The significance of the partridge is that it has a unique ringing-like call that can be heard loud and clear as it echoes above the mountains.[14]

I'm pointing out these phenomenal women because women's stories in the Bible are rarely told. More rare is that women are almost never named. But all FIVE women, five sisters are named. Therefore, when you come upon a story about a group who is rare yet who dare to challenge the status quo, you should take notice. The five sisters are older but bolder. They challenged the protocol by requesting to inherit their father's land and retain his name in their family clan. Their father, Zelophehad, was a son, but he had no sons. They lived in a time of patriarchal orthodox Judaism. Men were the decision-makers and history-makers; personal property decisions such as inheritances were all decided for men, with men, and by men. There were no roles for women outside of the home. Boys were celebrated and girls were tolerated. In other words, women were regulated to the sidelines. Numbers 27:1 lists the lineage of sons who preceded Zelophehad. It is implied that women were to be married to men and are, therefore, not significant in the genealogy. So, this story is extraordinary.

The five sisters (the first sorority!) found themselves in a crisis. What happens to the inheritance when there are no sons? No one had raised the question before, that is, until these dynamic women came along. Dr. Martin Luther King Jr. said, "The true measure of a man is not how he behaves in moments of comfort and convenience, but where he stands at times of controversy and challenge."[15] This culture had a crisis. These sisters faced a challenge and a controversy. Their father, the family patriarch, was dead, leaving behind five unmarried daughters and no sons. Unmarried women had a particular burden because men were seen as providers and protectors, while women were seen as property if no man were present. These five daughters of the deceased Zelophehad went from being invisible and without voice or choice to being visible and with strong voices. God affirmed that Zelophehad's daughters were right and should inherit their father's property. God also defined for Moses and the Israelites the proper lines of inheritance in a family clan and among the Israelites as a whole. Their daughters' right to inherit their father's property reflected what God had in mind for *all* women. These dynamic she-roes are a great influence in my life, and I hope their story will impact and affect yours as well.

Find Your Turning Point

An "aha moment" happened for the five sisters. After their father's death, they came alive. And so, my sisters, we have to put some things to death so that other things can live. It's only when some things are removed that new things can enter. Revelation 21:5a says, "Then he who sat on the throne said, 'Behold, I make all things new.'"

In addition, the prophet Isaiah had to wait until the death of King Uzziah *before* he saw the Lord and his transformation and real awakening took place (see Isaiah 6:1-10). In Acts 9:36-43 the story of Dorcas, as I interpret the text, I believe Dorcas died because she had surrounded herself with people, widows, some of whom were professional mourners, whose only mission in life was to go from funeral to funeral, grieving and weeping. Before the miracle of presenting her alive happened, the widows were taken out of the room. Darkness and light, nor death and life cannot be in the same space.

What chapters need to close in your life so that your "aha moment"—your turning point—can happen? Death and life can't exist in the same space or the same vessel. In Deuteronomy 30:19 Moses tells the Israelites to choose life or death. In my Fabulous Fifth Chapter, I choose life! Paul wrote to the Corinthians that in Christ the old things were gone, and all things were made new (see 2 Corinthians 5:17). Make this your *new* season to come *alive!* Don't wait until the changing of the calendar year. You can make the decision to start your new Fifth Chapter today. Come alive like the five daughters of Zelophehad!

Timing Is Everything

Zelophehad's daughters moved when the time was right. They were like a lyric in the hit song by Alicia Keys: those girls were "on fiya!" They knew the rules of their culture, and they put their life experiences to work and moved at the opportune time. Look at your Chapter Five as your opportune time to put to death the guilt, the shame, the burdens others have placed on you, and plan to make your move. Making your move not only means that you understand timing; it also means that you understand how to go about it, how to navigate, observe protocol, recognize who you need to speak with, and then make your move.

First, the sisters followed protocol and went to Moses (the leader); to Eleazar the priest (the spiritual leadership); to the princes (the royalty), and to all the congregation saying, "Our father died in the wilderness . . . and he had no sons. Why should the name of our father be removed from among his family because he had no son? Give us a possession among our father's brothers." (Numbers 27:3-4). In other words, "Give us our father's inheritance. Keep our legacy going." Moses took their cause before God, and God said to surely give the daughters the inheritance. God commanded a new statute to be drawn—to change the law books to reflect this new change (see Numbers 27:11).

An inheritance is what has been saved for you when the time is at hand. Do you know how much God has saved up for you, waiting for *you* to come and get it? In the world we say, "You go, girl!" or in Spanish, "Vaya, chica!" Rise up like these five sisters and go for it, all of it! Jesus said, "Ask, and it will be given to you; seek, and you will find; knock, and it will be opened to you" (Matthew 7:7).

Go and get the gifts God has for you. Act like, look like, walk like, talk like, and sound like a woman who is about to inherit *all* of it! You thought you were waiting for God, but God is waiting for you!

Paving the Way

Knowing your history is critical to making the right moves in your Fifth Chapter. The five sisters were fully aware of their lineage and financial plight. We can gain strength and wisdom when we understand the journey of our ancestors. As a child, my summers in the South were spent learning about my family's heritage. As a daughter born in the North, it meant that I had certain privileges my southern girl cousins didn't have, just by living in the "big city." Jobs were more plentiful in New York; therefore, my parents could make more money. Often, they would not only send *us* South; they would also send *money* to southern relatives to help them out. Fashion and music were centered in New York, so I had a certain "northern-ness" and boldness that my cousins did not have. Connecting to my mother's heritage in particular, where Black women could only become nurses or teachers to escape the rural sharecropping duties, was eye-opening. Watching her make her moves out of poverty into the middle class was inspiring.

My mom, my aunts, and their friends were "fly girls." They flew high and had fun in every season of their lives. They worked, saved, played, and partied. They all enjoyed being in each other's company, loved their families, and loved being around other people. I was fortunate to have a front-row seat because our house was the "hangout house." Most of the time, there was an eclectic group in our house, talking, eating, playing Bid Whist, and having clean fun that the entire intergenerational family could be involved with. My fifty-something parents attended a lot of house parties and dances, often given by churches. They'd reserve an entire table near where the bands would be playing. I watched as they did their hair and makeup and walked out the door. I saw them dress up, zip up one another's dresses, and dance the night away.

When I was in college, my mom was in her fifties. She loved interior decorating, and I would always come home to a renovated room or area of the house. Mom was an exceptional cook, and her dishes, especially during holidays, were plenteous, flavorful, and cultural, from our southern tradition. Mom and her friends traveled a lot, both nationally and internationally. On one occasion, she was in Ghana, West Africa, with an age fifty-plus Christian tour group at the same time I was there with a college group volunteering at Operation Crossroads Africa. I felt so proud to surprise her group and meet up with them. Talk about a moment of exuberant joy! There is nothing like a mother-daughter Motherland experience!

I can do a lot of Fifth Chapter things now that my mother could not do back then. She was born into the segregated South and a world of poverty. She worked her way up to middle class and then to wealth, but her road was not easy. Racism clipped her wings. Even though she was determined to do certain things and go to certain places, Jim Crow laws and segregation limited her. I valued all of the effort and journey my mother made to become an elementary school teacher. It was significant in everything I did going forward in life. My mother's name was Dorothy, and I truly am "Dorothy's daughter," a title I wear proudly. I walk like her, talk like her, and hold my head as she did. Coretta Scott King (my other mom) once wrote, "Before I was married to Martin and became a King, I was a proud Scott, shaped by my mother's discernment and my father's strength."[16]

Today, you and I are so fortunate to be able to grasp and hold onto our dreams, to seize—and even squeeze—

these precious moments now called our Fifth Chapter. I think what also makes Chapter Five so exciting is that we don't need to repeat the history of our ancestors, some of whom never got to do what they wanted to do or even imagine the things we're doing today. For many, if they worked, they stayed in "good government jobs," they received their gold watch, stayed alive for a few years after retirement, and then they died. But understand that we stand on their shoulders, which means we can do things they were never able to do and go places they could not go—or even contemplate going.

The Fifth Chapter is a leap that many women who preceded us could not reach. My late parents were strong. They had to be sharecroppers in their generation, but they knew that was neither their destiny nor mine. They built a life that allowed me to go farther and faster, and be fiercer than they ever experienced. So, in my Fifth Chapter, I'm thankful for their past sacrifices. And now, I'm ready to *soar*. I want more. I'm ready to be fabulously fulfilled.

Recently I had dinner with some women who are all in their late fifties. We initially met when our children started pre-K together, so that has been a while. One woman always wanted to go to nursing school, so she did. While her son was off at college, she did all her coursework, internships, and rotations, and finally became a licensed RN in a hospital she loved. Now that her son, her only child, has graduated and is doing well on his own, she has remarried and bought a house in Oregon, where she has always wanted to live. She is enjoying her life more than ever. She timed her move and made it steady and on point. As Ecclesiastes 3:1-2 says, "To everything there is a season, A time for every purpose under heaven: A time to be born, and a time to die; A time to plant, and a time to pluck what is planted." In other words, seeds are sown in planting but seeds also grow, and the five sisters had grown with the seeds of faith planted deeply within them. You, too, my sisters, have had five-plus decades of growth, and if you'll examine how seeds have grown in your own life, and where you've "harvested their crops," it will be enlightening. Isn't that what the psalmist declared in Psalm 1:3? "He shall be like a tree Planted by the rivers of water, That brings forth its fruit in its season, Whose leaf also shall not wither; And whatever he does shall prosper."

The actions of Zelophehad's daughters were remarkable. Life-changing, in fact. Their move changed the course of history. The laws were changed to reflect gender equality. They stood tall and withstood societal landmines, pitfalls, and sinkholes. When they arrived on the scene, they made an entrance, not in an arrogant way, but with confidence. What's holding you back? Timing is everything. Make your move and don't look back. Do a two-step, snap your fingers, throw your head back, and sing a feel-good tune, like McFadden and Whitehead's "Ain't No Stoppin' Us Now!"

Your Next Move: Your Turning Point Exercise

What moves have you always wanted to make?

What were your excuses?

What can you do now to make those moves?

CHAPTER THREE

Yours for the Taking

*"We don't stop playing because we grow old;
we grow old because we stop playing."*
—George Bernard Shaw[17]

It was not only reading about the five daughters of Zelophehad that moved me. It was also reading a story in the Gospel of John that stirred my soul. Jesus performed a miracle on a man who had been sitting in the same position by the pool of Bethesda for thirty-eight years. Researchers believe that there were two parts to this five-porched pool where Jesus would also take his ritual baths. On one side were the healing waters, while the other side had running water to continually refresh and replenish the water. When Jesus came by, he saw everyone else getting their opportunity for healing while this man sat and watched. It appears that the man's paralysis was not only physical but also emotional, spiritual, and mental, and prevented him from doing whatever it took to get in. Instead, he made excuses, and his words to Jesus were, "Sir, I have no man to put me into the pool when the water is stirred up; but while I am coming, another steps down before me" (John 5:7).

My sisters, what are you waiting for to soar? Have you been waiting for someone to carry you? Have you been seeing everyone soar or run past you in the last five decades? Well, don't be *sore* anymore, it's your time to soar! No one will carry you into your Fifth Chapter. You can be your own architect and build this chapter the way you'd like it to be. You can add all the bells and whistles, or just chill out. Either way, the healing waters have always been there—waiting for you to own up to the areas of your life you want to work on. And the replenishing waters as well—they've been flowing, waiting for you to "rise, take up your mat and walk" (John 5:8).

Take Up Your Mat

Your mat represents the old you, the you that was stuck in one place. You are not there anymore. Just by reading this book, you've chosen to see what options might be available for you. Don't leave any vestiges of the past because they only get in your way. Today is your new day! As Scripture says, "This *is* the day the LORD has made; we will rejoice and be glad in it" (Psalm 118:24). At some point, you have to stop feeling sorry for yourself, stop looking at where you are with self-pity or piety, and start looking for the plenty and the party. Let the good times roll! The man at the pool was a solo, self-doubting, self-destructive person. Just think if the daughters of Zelophehad would have let their circumstances cause them to focus on a history that was not affirming of women, or if they turned that history into hysteria. They would have missed what God wanted for them all along. Navigating this lie of life means just that—getting up from the pools that have been filled with "I can't" and turn them into "I can!"

To navigate is the opposite of to negate. You pull out all the yeses in your heart and mind and soul and say to yourself, "I'm going for it. No matter what age. No matter what stage. I will not be defeated by depression, a diagnosis, a detour, nor a distraction. I'm aiming for the bull's-eye." As the late Dr. Katie G. Cannon, womanist theologian extraordinaire, said to me, "You have to let the yes-es line up." When I was waiting for an affirmative Senate confirmation vote, I waited until the yes-es lined up. Believe me, as you know by now, the world is filled with no's. But you must find your yes. Don't stop until you get a yes. Like David, a shepherd boy in his father's field, he watched all his brothers line up to be examined for the kingdom by King Saul. But then God said, "There's still another whom I've anointed. You've only tapped into seven brothers. But there's one more—whom I have chosen" (1 Samuel 16:11-12, paraphrased). There's no doubting that God has great things in store for you. God offers you "a future and a hope" (Jeremiah 29:11). Turn any negative thought, comment, or no into a yes. Even if there are seven others (or more) who go before you, your yes will come. Stop negating. Start navigating, initiating and anticipating your blessed Fabulous Fifth Chapter.

My DE-SMOGG Principles™

Sometimes our lives are clouded by the issues and troubles that distract us or cloud our vision. Johnny Nash's song, "I Can See Clearly Now" reminds us that "rain" does come, and it will dissipate. I have created an acronym I call the DE-SMOGG Principles™. Smog is where haze and fog meet, and one cannot see her way. Yet to DE-SMOGG™ is to understand how to make things work for you and how to have clarity in this fifth season of life. For me, I had to relocate for a season to change from the fast, frantic pace of inner-city New York. I was recovering from a grueling congressional campaign and from raising two sons on a single income. I chose to relocate to a slower, calmer pace on the waterfront of Washington, DC. I still kept my apartment, house, and doctors in New York, but I needed a balance from the stress. It was in my *balance* time, which I call "selah"— the biblical term used to pause in the Psalms. I believe that God gave me these DE-SMOGG™ Principles. It was a revealing time when God wiped the fog, smog, and haze away from my life. It's never too late to have an eye-opening revelation. Think about it. Isaiah the prophet had his eyes opened. Blind Bartimaeus had his eyes opened. Deborah sat under her palm tree, and I— "Sujay"—sat in my big red chair on the Potomac River on the DC waterfront, napping when I wanted, and sleeping when I wanted, being with whom I wanted, and how I wanted with friends whom I wanted to be around. You'll be surprised what a little refreshing will do, and when you embrace DE-SMOGG™ and live it out, you will be armed with the right mindset to make your next bold move.

So what is DE-SMOGG™?

D = DIGITIZE: Grab hold of the divine power within you and learn to go digital and virtual. Little did we know that COVID-19 would come and catch us, knocking us off our feet. Those who understand technology and how to attend meetings and see family and friends online were ahead of the game. I know nursing home patients who were able to communicate with their loved ones because of AARP's GrandPad (a special tablet that has larger letters and an intuitive interface). To be able to progress, communicate, and accelerate during a pandemic or separation, we need to digitize.

E = ENERGIZE: When you hold on to God, you will have the energy you need to go into this chapter and the next. Energy always precedes synergy and synchronicity. God is getting ready to DE-SMOGG™ your life.

S = STRATEGIZE: Do not move forward without a clear strategy or plan for this phase of your life. Even to do nothing, to retire, or to hang out, you need a plan. The five daughters were waiting for the opportune time. Yet while they were waiting, they were also anticipating their moment to move following the proper protocol. I'd also like to think they were calculating the cost of living without a man in the house. Have you counted up your costs to make your move?

M = MONETIZE: No one, man or woman, can live by bread alone. You need to have your funds in order for at least six months of expenses. This amount includes salary, benefits, travel, and meals, plus extra stashed away for a rainy day. You can say, "It's raining right now—raining life, raining joy, and raining retirement. This is my rainy day, and I have enough to cover me until I decide to do something more. I was speaking with J.B., a woman about to turn sixty. She has not only saved up for retirement but also for a big sixtieth birthday bash, as well as a nice rental home back in her birthplace, which she enjoys visiting regularly. While others her age are taking the "buyout" or retirement package, she has chosen to wait until her youngest son graduates from college, to continue working, then get a side contract and hang in there for another ten years to get her full retirement and full social-security benefits.

J.B.'s plan doesn't have to be your plan, but you must have a plan that is economically feasible and fabulously prepares you to "coast" into your Fifth Chapter. If you aren't ready right now, don't be so hard on yourself. Create a plan to slowly work towards your goal. Work smarter, not harder. There are all kinds of financial planning tools available these days, and you may want to start with AARP.

O = ORGANIZE: Put your life in order. Organize your thoughts, your closets, your surroundings. It's called de-cluttering, throwing away, cleaning your surroundings. I had 154 boxes on my last de-cluttering project! That's crazy, you may say, but since I worked for high-level government for so many years, I couldn't just throw pages and pages away. Many of them contained personal and classified information. So, I had to wait until the right time to dispose of the documents, as well as the time when I had time and energy. It took a while, but I had a plan to empty box by box.

I imagine that you also may have accumulated quite a bit in your life, some for your profession, medical records for you and your family. Of course, all of these things were necessary at the time. But do you remember what I wrote about the season? When circumstances change, such as the death of a loved one, kids growing up and moving out, or moving to a smaller space, your mindset has to shift. All of these are great moments to refocus and reorganize your life and your thoughts, which will allow you to see major results.

G = GLOBALIZE: Moving forward means "getting off your block" and beginning to see a world that's huge. When I had 199 countries in my portfolio, there was no looking back. Yes, I am just a girl from the Bronx, but now I'm a woman on the world stage. My final trip with the State Department was to Nigeria. It happened to be over my fifty-fifth birthday. I asked myself, *Where would you like to be on your fifty-fifth birthday?* I had spent two summers in Ghana in my college years and longed to go back. I could not think of anything to top a birthday in Ghana, so that's what I did. After my side trip from Nigeria to Ghana was approved, I bought my ticket, met the U.S. ambassador to Ghana, and stayed with a girlfriend, Michelle McKinney Hammond. We attended church at the Ghanian Cathedral, under the leadership of Archbishop Duncan Williams, and then my friends threw me a party overlooking a beautiful part of Accra, a city I learned to love while living there. In addition, I believe my ancestry is from that country.

In 2019 I attended the Women on the Worldstage (W.O.W.) Conference in Bali as part of our international women's exchange. In making my reservations, I treated myself to business class on Turkish Air, where a chef came out and asked, "How would you like your eggs cooked?" Then the flight attendant came and made my bed-in-the-air so that I could stretch out and rest. My trip ended with a roundtable of indigenous, interfaith, and expat women, all working and praying together, in a circle of love. Girl, I encourage you to take your wings and fly!

G = GLAMORIZE: Wherever you go, always look the part. Sister, author, and Delta Sigma Theta Sorority sister Paula Giddings penned a book entitled *When and Where I Enter*, in which she describes the path of several influential African American women who opened doors and paved the way for political and social change for the rest of our sisters to enter. Whatever doors you'd like to enter at this stage of life, feel free to do so, but be ready!

Do you remember when we played "dress up" as little girls? I recall it like it was yesterday—putting on my mom's big high-heel shoes, red lipstick, and scarf over my "gown." I loved looking at myself in the mirror all dressed up, imagining the places I could go. As a child, I had no idea I would have the opportunity to travel the globe. What a true blessing! Now in my fabulous Fifth Chapter, I'm going everywhere I want to go, dressing up, sometimes with bling, other times with pearls, and having a ball.

Your Next Move: Yours for the Taking Exercise
Using the DE-SMOGG Principles™, map out where you
stand in each area and your plan to move you to where
you want to be.

D = Digitize

E = Energize

S = Strategize

M = Monetize

O = Organize

G = Globalize

G = Glamorize

CHAPTER FOUR

Five Fabulous Lessons

"You can't go back and change the beginning, but you can start where you are and change the ending."—C. S. Lewis[18]

Not only did I learn from the Biblical fabulous daughters of Zelophehad; I also learned from the man at Bethesda's pool. I think that's why life is so exciting—we can learn from each other's experiences, and it's not gender exclusive. As we are walking through this Fifth Chapter of our lives, we must be continuous learners as well as share our knowledge and lessons to help our sisters make smart, strategic moves and avoid the pitfalls that we ourselves have made.

Fabulous Lesson One: Fierce and Fulfilled
During the 2019 Golden Globe Award Show, Glenn Close accepted the award for best actress in a motion picture, The Wife, saying that the film had taken fourteen years to make. The film is about a wife named Joan who followed behind and deferred to her husband, Joseph, throughout their marriage. He accepts the Nobel Prize in Literature for his superb accomplishments, even though Joan actually rewrote and improved his best-selling novel and a number of his other publications.

In her acceptance speech, Close said, "I'm thinking of my mom, who sublimated herself to my father her whole life, and in her eighties she said to me, 'I feel like I haven't accomplished anything, and it's just not right. Do all you want to do. You should have the life you want.'" Speaking directly to the women in the audience, Close also said: "We have to find personal fulfillment. We have to follow our dreams. We have to say, 'I can do that and I should be allowed to do that.'"[19]

This, my sisters, is the key to what Chapter Five is all about. Whatever you said you wanted to do, try it. Do it. At this writing, I'm taking standup comedy classes, something I've always wanted to do. Comedy helped me through the rough days of being on the front lines of 9/11 "Ground Zero" as an NYPD chaplain, and at other monumental moments in my life. Laughter has a way of calming the soul. I intend to laugh, dance, and sing my way through the rest of my Chapter Five.

> *"One of the lessons that I grew up with was to always stay true to yourself and never let what somebody else says distract you from your goals."*—Michelle Obama[20]

Single and Satisfied
I met a new girlfriend, Denise, who helps women of all ages with "Dating, Mating and Relating." So many have tried the online dating route but found that it was just not relational enough. Many have opted for celibacy singleness and are satisfied with it. It takes a lot to really own where we are sexually, after fifty. For some, their libido is way hot.

Others have formed almost a mystic, contemplative approach, where they are fulfilled in their singleness. One of my "80 something" friends says I dare and "have a spare" (boyfriend) at all times. There is no one approach: whether it's hiring people like Denise as matchmakers and dating coaches, or going online, it is a process that is very involved. You must declare in your heart, mind, and spirit that you're alright being single and satisfied with it and will not allow others to force you. You're willing to "wait on God," in your singleness, and you don't feel you're walking alone but you're walking with him and in him.

Not Single and Not Satisfied

Then there are others, especially over fifty, who may have married young and realized they are no longer "in love" with their spouse and are not satisfied in their relationship. So, what's a woman to do? My sixty-something girlfriend said, "I got a good therapist to talk with regularly. She's helping me through this mess." Another immediately filed for divorce and began working with a life coach to find out what she really wanted to do with her life. She started out being a healthy-lifestyle coach, then earned her RN degree, and is now a fabulous nurse. She used this season to find the true "desires of her heart." Bishop John and Rev. Cecelia Williams Bryant, after 53 years of holy matrimony, have a new book for Christians who really want to stay in COVENANT relationship.

Here's the thing: It's challenging. And not a lot of pastors openly deal with it, so many receive their info from the "sex therapists," who are not Christian. And many of us in the Christian faith really do ourselves a disservice when we say, "You must be equally yoked. It is referring to not being connected with the darkness of this world, but rather surrounding yourselves with like-minded delivers in Christ, in and out of marriages. Well, if you're both Christians but not equally yoked in society, or in the practice of your faith, or in education, then you're not equally yoked. If you're a college graduate and your spouse is not, chances are at some point you will grow apart. You'll run out of things to talk about, and he or she may not have any frame of reference for your thoughts and conversation. Sometimes blue-collar and white-collar marriages work, but socioeconomic influences can be distracting and destructive. As you get older, you have less tolerance to overlook certain things.

Here is what I want to emphasize: stop being so hard on yourself. The twenty-something or thirty-something woman who got married was a different woman from the forty-, fifty-, or sixty-year-old. I have a dear sister, a pastor friend, who had stayed married with her "photo op" husband, although they hadn't shared a bed for the past twenty years, and she finally said, "Look, let's move on amicably." They did, and she remarried, has a house and a husband at home that she loves, and who loves her, and she is enjoying their pool and puppies. Many people are staying in places and relationships which are literally hurting, destroying, or killing them. It's important, if you can, for all parties involved, to seek help through Christian therapy and mediation, but if you feel there's harm to your body or your soul, it may be time to move on. I'm advocating for fulfillment, peace. Sometimes folks are not "equally yoked," and if outside help cannot help, then both should leave with, and in peace. You should not suffer with pain, heartaches, and headaches. Can I get a witness?

Fabulous Lesson Two: Faith

God Can Supersize Blessings

Everyone can be blessed. No one's gender, race, or ethnicity motivates God to do more for one than the other. And if we ever needed to hear and know that this is a time in American history, where there is no superior, nor inferior, person nor race. In fact, when I think of blessings, I recall a term I heard when I was flipping the TV channels and caught Joel Osteen, the well-known televangelist pastor from Houston, Texas. He described the huge blessings that are waiting for us as "explosive," beyond measure. Sometimes I use the word "explosive" and other times I use a slogan from McDonald's—I believe God "can supersize" blessings. In fact, in Paul's letter to the church at Ephesus, 3:12, he says, "God can do exceedingly, abundantly above all that we ask...." (NKJV). I believe that even sometimes when we don't ask, God shows up and blesses beyond measure. I believe God rewards faithfulness. When we've been "at it" for some time, there are gifts and blessings that await us. As Hebrews 11:1 reminds us, "Faith is the substance of things hoped for, the evidence of things not seen." You may not be able to see the blessings coming with your eyes, but in your spirit, you know they are on the way. It's important to keep and hold on to that NOW faith, which means that in the present, see what's going to manifest for you. Some have a vision board. I say ask God for a vision.

When I arrived as senior pastor of my first church, Mariners' Temple, things didn't look so good. There was a huge building that needed repair There were very few parishioners, all in their Fifth Chapter of life, and no treasury. But we remained faithful— the followers and I, focused and faithful, and God rewarded our faithfulness. Mariners' Temple was able to become a magnet church that drew folks from all over the city and neighboring states.

Stand by the Door

The daughters of Zelophehad stood by the door of the tabernacle to ask for their inheritance. The door of the tabernacle is the equivalent of a sanctuary for us in a faith community. It's a faith center where we collectively and individually gather to worship and to honor God.

Don't be so busy doing PowerPoint that you forget where the real point of power comes from. Remember that, as Christian women, we have a secret weapon: the power of faith and the power of prayer. "The effective, fervent prayer of the righteous . . . avails much" (James 5:16, NKJV). In Hebrews 10:25 we are told not to forsake "the assembling of ourselves together." Faith communities and places of worship are not only sacred; they are often our survival. It is not in the ordinary but in the extraordinary that God moves, whether digitally or in person. FBC (First Baptist Church of Glenarden International) now has an online campus community, bringing six continents together.

I can't tell you how often I have to pull out this weapon of prayer when things get rough and tough, especially in the world of politics and in senior levels of government. Prayer is the chief navigator. It's like the navigation system in your car that steers you in the right direction, "GPS" (God's Protective Services). That's what prayer does for the believer. The compass and everything else could be telling you to go another way, but prayer unlocks the door; it is the very key to the kingdom. And the good thing about prayer is that other women can join in with you and pray for you. Just like folks have book clubs, you can have a prayer club. It can be formal or informal, in person or via technology, such as FaceTime or Zoom. Or it can be to go into your prayer closet alone and talk with Jesus. We can say whatever is on our minds or whisper softly, Jesus will hear us and answer our prayers. Celvant Derricks wrote about how Jesus is a great prayer listener in his song, "Just a Little Talk with Jesus." So, gather and put your prayer requests before God and one another, and then have someone just start praying. Pray for your needs, your enemies, and how to handle the new ages and stages of life that you're going through, whether large or small, and you will have victory. Remember Psalm 23:5, tells us that "God prepares a table before us in the presence of our enemies."

Have "Village" Sisters

My faith community and my "village" of sisters have been extremely important to me. Having the First Baptist Church of Glenarden International (Maryland), Pastor John K. Jenkins and his family, my home church, Union Baptist Church in the village of Harlem, and my prayer warrior sisters available to pray for and with me has been so meaningful. When days got rough and tough, I knew I could find solace in the faith community and in the comfort of friends and extended family.

Stand Strong in Your Faith

Stand strong in your faith. Whatever your life looked like is in the past, and there's always hope for a brighter future. Lest we forget, Jeremiah 29:11 says, "God has plans for you, not for you to be defeated but to prosper in every way." One definition of *prosper* is to gain and flourish, especially in the area of finances. However, other translations of the Hebrew word are *welfare* and *peace*. In any case, God is opening the door for you to walk through to discover His future plans for you.

Fabulous Lesson Three: Fiscal and Physical Fitness

"Fine, Fit, and Fabulous" is an initiative I created when I was in my third decade of pastoring in inner-city New York. The weight of life had caused me, and many women in my congregation, to add a lot of weight to our frames. I first noticed it as people would approach the altar to bring their tithes and offerings. Women, mainly in their fifties or older, were having a difficult time walking, and some were even gasping for breath. We all needed some new discipline in our lives that would take us from the younger years to and through the more seasoned ones. I wanted my fifty-and-over sisters to live! When I played basketball in school and things were in disarray on the court, my coach would call a "time out." God, I believe, was coaching me to call a "time out."

Health Makeover

In a few months, we as a congregation lost several hundred pounds and lots of inches. Then, after some guidance and coaching from professionals, and a larger community effort, we were successful in losing more weight and living a healthier lifestyle. As a public figure who traveled quite a bit, I had to be even more deliberate with myself because my increase in age and increase in weight combined were becoming cumbersome.

This is the stage in life where you have to put everything in check. Even if you worked out in your thirties, forties, and fifties; even if you were a star athlete, even if you walked every day—your body changes. Your metabolism, figure, skin, cells, hormones—everything changes! So, the sooner you put your physical house in order, the better and longer you'll live.

At one point, I had to go to five different doctors. No longer do we go into one waiting room, see one doctor, and leave with a clear diagnosis and prescription. Now, you go to your primary-care doctor, who does your checkup, finds something, sends you to the specialist because he or she wants to make sure that the specialist does not find any serious issues. The specialist orders more tests and X-rays. Those tests are sent to a radiologist, and to your primary-care doctor, who may want another set of tests. One checkup can lead to weeks of doctors' appointments. Fifth Chapter healthcare is no joke!

The joy of navigating life in the Fifth Chapter is that you can take charge, take control, and still have a great quality of life if you take care of yourself, get your medical checkups, stay active, and take precautions. Twenty to thirty minutes of exercise per day can make a drastic difference in your mobility. My youngest son, the jock, says, "Mom, you're more active than most of your friends, but you can still do a little more in the fitness arena." That's a major statement coming from my twenty-something son. He observes that women around me are not very active and is concerned. He also knows that I can do more.

As I shared in an earlier chapter, I am a swimmer. I try to stay close to or near an indoor pool. I also request a place with an indoor pool when I travel so I can keep up my routine. When I led my "Selah by the Sea" retreat, I had a room with not only a pool view but easy access. I find that now more than ever, when I'm in the water, I meet God. So, it's a spiritual experience for me as well as a fitness activity. During that retreat, I swam twice a day, every day, for at least thirty minutes before and after our sessions. I built in break time for attendees in the middle of the day, for at least six hours, so that they could enjoy the resort and environment that they paid for. I cannot tell you how great I felt at the end of the week, even with all the responsibilities on my shoulders. I felt great both physically and emotionally. I could even see that the contour of my body had changed. This experience motivated me to weigh myself, make better food choices, and keep exercising in order to feel my best physically, emotionally, and spiritually.

Wealth Makeover

> *"Lasting net worth comes only when you have a healthy and strong sense of self-worth."*
> —Suze Orman[21]

All my life I was told to "save for a rainy day." Most likely, you were, too—or are familiar with the phrase. Well, consider it raining now!

First of all, of course being "fiscally fit" has many benefits. Many of you may not have a great past regarding your finances. The way you saved in the past will determine the quality of life and lifestyle you'll have now. But no matter what age you are, it is not too late to put some money away or rearrange your assets. Commonly held advice is that you should have at least six months of savings to cover your expenses. That's "liquid money," which means you can get to it in a hurry if you need to. Disclaimer: I am not a financial planner or a wealth investment advisor. I can only tell you what's worked for me.

If you have money saved up, you can really start tackling your "bucket list." Sit down with a financial planner first and ask about when and how to annuitize those "spending monies," and give yourself an "allowance." Go to the places that you can afford because you did what you had to do and deserve to reap your reward.

I boast to my friends that I am the "frugal queen." Having had two sons in private school, and then college and grad school at the same time, I had to learn how to not just survive but to thrive. I learned to take my own lunch on a plane in order to avoid airport food and prices. I have no shame in putting food in baggies and making my own trail mix. Now I can eat whatever I want when I want because I saved whenever I could. I can go wherever I want because I pulled back when necessary. Get serious about your health and finances in order to make this Fifth Chapter one to remember.

Fabulous Lesson Four:
Personal and Financial Freedom

You are finally free. No diapers for children (but sometimes, as older adults, you may have to wear them!). No more tuition payments or trips to the warehouse club. My **faith** now intersects with my **fun,** and I have the **funds** to do what I need to do. I am **financially free!** And that's fabulous! I didn't just save for a rainy day. I saved for a sunny day! Financial freedom means so many things: the ability to make choices, the ability to drown out unhealthy voices, the ability to walk, run, play, travel, and leave a legacy.

In the past, women used to save money in a cookie jar, (or in their bras) usually for emergencies, or to purchase something for their kid's school needs. One of the reasons I was able to move into Chapter Five so easily was that I had a year's savings to cover a year's worth of everything—bills, tuition, food, and rent. It took a number of years to amass this amount, but it was there right on time when I needed it the most.

Here are a few tips, leading up to an arrival at Chapter Five:

1. Meet with a reputable financial planner—one referred by friends who have accelerated their funds—and let your monies work for you.

2. Save at least half of every paycheck. I like this formula: tithe 10 percent to God, put 10 percent away for your kids and 10 percent for bills, and then put half of the remaining 70 percent in savings or other interest-bearing account.

3. Make sure you have an updated Last Will and Testament, as well as a Living Will, should your family have to make tough medical decisions on your behalf. Be clear on what you'd like to leave to whom and what you'd like done if you become incapacitated and after you die.

4. From your accumulated funds, take 10 percent per year and have some fun.

5. Purchase long-term insurance so you'll be able to live comfortably in your old age without burdening your children.

No Vows of Poverty

Somewhere in the psyche or cultures of many minorities, civil servants, and nonprofit leaders is the notion, communicated overtly and subtly, that you should never have "too much" money. Make enough to make ends meet, and don't worry about saving, just be thankful for what you have. In the end, many of us die broke, busted, and disgusted, because we never had enough to do the things we wanted to do. We "make do," as my southern relatives would say, but they really weren't "making it." Whether you're in ministry, nonprofit, or any other world, you must make a profit. We live in a capitalistic society, and the economic engine keeps running, whether you're putting gas in the engine (or in this case, cash) or not. You must have more than when you began; otherwise, you are an indentured servant. You must be able to not only make ends meet but far surpass that, with "dream money" to live out your dreams.

You also need to save for unexpected expenses, as this thing called "life" can sometimes sneak up on you. For example, there was a flood in my brand-new apartment caused by a building malfunction. Thankfully, I was covered by both my building and renter's insurance, but in the meantime, while I was waiting for the process to play out, I had to live, and so I needed to have those funds readily available until my reimbursement came through. One of the reasons I left government when I did, even at the senior level, was because many of my international expenses were out-of-pocket, and then I had to wait weeks for reimbursement. Well, bills don't have a waiting date. They have a "due date." To the extent possible, we must know our cash flow. That's why they call it a "flow." If it's not flowing, you're in a financial mess.

Alone but Not Lonely

Please don't be afraid to eat alone. Don't be afraid to be alone. I recall hearing a speech by Gwendolyn Goldsby Grant, formerly of *Essence* magazine, and I'm paraphrasing, but she said, "Don't say I'm having dinner **by** myself. Say I'm having dinner **with** myself."[22] Let me tell you something, sisters: there's nothing like getting your favorite food and just enjoying it, not having to share it, or having anyone judge you for it.

You can travel alone. There are so many amazing things to do, to see, and you'll find you are not out there alone. Today, more than ever, there are single women who can help you navigate Fifth Chapter travel on a shoestring budget, with a backpack, and who can tell you where you can get the best hairdressers and stylists for your texture of hair.

I love Christmas in New York City. Rockefeller Center becomes so magical. But I also love a good New York slice of pizza—there's nothing like it in the world! This past Christmas, I jumped off the subway at Rockefeller Center and I got the gooiest slice of pizza. As the cheese ran down off the pizza all over my face, I just giggled with glee, like a little kid eating a Christmas candy cane. I was so satisfied, so happy, so free. Free to just be me. No one there knew me. No one saw me—and even if they did, it was okay since I was enjoying MY slice of pizza. I had given myself permission to be gooey and enjoy what I had been missing. Nowhere in the world, in my opinion, makes pizza like NYC. It's my hometown and it's one of my hometown's favorite food. It makes grown folks giddy.

I really enjoy being alone in New York City during the holiday season. When our children were small, we would actually check into a hotel in midtown, as though we were tourists, and enjoy our own city: the skating rink, the hot chocolate, the store windows, and the Salvation Army Santas on the street corners. But now, they have their own adventures during the holidays, with other millennials, on the beach and in the city of Miami, or skiing in the Alps. We try to have Thanksgiving and Christmas Day dinner together, but I don't have to share all the days leading up to those special family celebrations.

Intergenerational Transference of Wealth
I want to speak with you about not just money for the present, or down the road, but for the years after we're gone. Perhaps you don't have children, but your funds can speak for you and help another generation who will follow. You can give to your church, your denomination,

or a nonprofit, in order to continue the work that you are passionate about. You can give to a college, whether it's your alma mater or not, or a school that has values and goals that you support, or to an institution that offers STEM scholarships to young urban girls, or to your favorite charity. In this way, another generation benefits from your knowledge, expertise, and willingness to spread your funds to do good. There's a politically correct term for it now: "social impact." There are stockbrokers and wealth managers who will invest only in sustainable, social impact funds, so not only are your dollars growing; they are also sowing into good soil, to do good in this world. The bottom line is to leave something for the next generation. Even if you are not here to see it, your legacy will live on.

Fabulous Lesson Five: Fun

I was a pre-Title IX woman, which meant we had to play "girls' basketball," with limited roles, and did not receive sports scholarships as today's female athletes do. I loved basketball, so I learned from some of the best basketball players on the planet: the teenage guys who played "b-ball" in the New York City parks. I'd sit for hours on park benches outside the fence just watching them. At some point they tired of me just watching, and they'd throw the ball to me and say, "Baby girl" (a term of affection in the city), if you want to have fun and play this game, then you've got to get *in* the game." Well, your Fifth Chapter says, "I'm ready to get in the game, without looking through the fence, or sitting on the bench and without coaching. I know

who I am and I know what I want—and I know it's
time to get in and play!"

Happy Hour
Pre-COVID, I decided that, in the past, I've lived everywhere that was convenient for my kids' schools and
playdates, or for our offices. But my kids are adults
now, so I made a move for ME!! I declared it was MY
turn. It wasn't a senior assisted living facility, although
some may want to choose that, nor was it a gated community, but it was with which I had familiarity, and
where I could have fun, with a community and extended "family" and friends. I moved to an apartment
complex in a newly renovated area, that's very much
like an adult Disney World or day camp for adults,
where my neighbors and I have pure fun—all the time
and many of my best friends lived right across the street,
("the Waterside crew" cited previously in the Acknowl-
edgments). Every week is a new adventure. As new
restaurants open, there are grand opening events, so we
go out to restaurants, for breakfast, brunch and dinner,
theater, games, swimming pools, and parties. We enjoy
being together. We laugh. We dance and have fun without having to be "on." Being the nation's Capital, the
DC area is used to loads of public figures, so there's
room for anonymity, if you're always on the front lines.
If you are public figures, or "out front" most of the
time, it's important for you to have places where there's
no judgment and no expectations of performance. We
call it our "safe space." Many of us are, or have been,
public figures, or are accomplished at the top of our

games, such as military brass, where every move made has been watched closely, and where there was always a dress code or protocol to follow. But now, collectively, like the daughters of Zelophehad, we travel in a "pack of five," and we're the "five alive." We look out for one another. We hang together, we grieve together, we celebrate our milestones and those of our families, and we know when each of us needs to be left alone. It's a rare gift, to find friends with whom you can age, and who love you at any stage.

Travel

The psalmist declares that "the earth is the LORD's and the fullness thereof; the world, and they that dwell therein" (Psalm 24:1, KJV). Loosely translated, this means that everything on the planet belongs to the Lord, so no matter where you go, you can have a faith experience. Whether it's an overnight girls trip nearby, or whether you've saved up for that lifetime girls' trip to Bali, or one of your favorite nearby destinations, if you're ready, willing and able, just do it! Visit this wonderful world that God has given us. Tourism and hospitality all over the world have become so good at it, that they customize a tour or a trip on low budgets, or if you wish, a larger one. For a trip I took to Bali with six women, they were not rich women, but they had a dream and had been saving all their lives to go there. But certainly, trips don't have to be far, nor extravagant. Post-COVID, even a trip to the next county will do wonders. Money and costs do not define your travel. You start out with your dreams, and then go for it!!

Pajamas in the Bahamas

I'm enjoying my Fifth Chapter. It's my "coming out" party. I'm coming out of the shadows into the marvelous light. I recall a commercial I saw on TV a few years ago for a luxury car whose motto was "where my new life meets my new lifestyle." That's where I am—I'm a little older, a little wiser, and not afraid to have some good old fun. I remember so vividly that when I was a young single woman, I would take a Bahamas Air flight out of New York City directly to Nassau, meet friends for lunch and an afternoon together, and then catch the return flight in the evening. It was so much fun! Over the years, I also made many other friends there who were also single. Later, many of us married and had children who grew up together. I also had childhood friends who I went to camp with; their father was Bahamian, and after high school, they moved there. It's awesome to rekindle old relationships, as well as to see the Bahamas or other country "like a native" by going to the local churches, dining in the Arawak Cay (where fresh fish and conch were served daily) and enjoying the nightlife and beautiful beaches. The best part of vacationing is there's no alarm clock and no hard timeline, so you can plan accordingly.

No Pain in Spain

When I was fifteen, I lived in Valencia, Spain, as part of a study-abroad program. Now, with the numbers in my age reversed, (fifty-one and then some) I'd like to revisit some of the places I went to while there. When a TV commercial shows the "running of the bulls," my memory immediately goes back to those teenage days when I was fresh and vibrant, immersed in and learning about a new culture. How marvelous it would be to go back there, for either business or pleasure.

Back to the Motherland

If you're still working and are fortunate enough to get an overseas assignment or trip, I encourage you to "go global." If there's time, when someone else is paying for your trip, plan a few days before or after just to enjoy the local culture outside your hotel.

DNA testing makes it a wonderful time to reconnect and re-bond with one's history. The year 2020 marked the four-hundredth anniversary of forced enslavement of Africans to the Americas. Instead of speaking about the "point of no return"—the point where Africans knew it was too late to try to return home—many African Americans now speak about the "point of return." Thousands of African Americans, including members of the Congressional Black Caucus, have returned to the "motherland." Millennials have organized and embarked on trips to various countries in Africa to learn their history and to pay homage to their ancestors.

Don't overlook amazing history trips to visit some of the "wonders of the world," such as the pyramids in Egypt or Petra in Jordan. In this Fifth Chapter, you don't have to just read about these wonders; you can touch, feel, see, and experience some of the most awesome sights in this world. Consider taking a ride on a riverboat down the Nile. Start putting your checklist together and double check that you have a valid passport, which usually means that it can't expire less than six months *after* your trip. Check with the rules of the country or countries you plan to visit for more information.

Dance Like It's 1999

When one of the attendees at my retreats, whom we've affectionately called "DJ Tish," (a pre-Fifth Chapter DJ), pulls out her playlist of dancing music, the pure fun begins. Tish plays music from all eras that are bound to make you want to get your groove on. Everyone gets up and makes their moves—the attendees, the presenters, the Americans, and those from overseas. Music and dancing become our universal language.

After God miraculously parted the Red Sea and allowed the Israelites to escape from the Egyptians, what did the people do? Moses, Aaron, the men, and the women all began to dance, thanking God for this new beginning, this next chapter of their journey. Miriam and the women pulled out their tambourines to accompany their dance. Doesn't Psalm 150 remind us that everything that has breath can praise God with instruments, with cymbals, and with dance? That means using every part of us, every instrument available to us. So, pull out your tambourines and dance, my friends!

Your Next Move: Fabulous Lessons Exercise
Which lesson(s) resonated with you and why?

CHAPTER FIVE

It's Your Time and Your Turn

This is not just a bedtime storybook for you to imagine what someone else might do. It really *is* your turn, so let this be your defining moment. Start making your list. Who am I? Who do I want to be? Who am I not? Think of all the things you've ever thought of doing. Remember that dreams do not have an expiration date nor an age limit. What will it take to get there? Don't overthink this. Don't make it complicated. Jesus said, "I have come that they may have life, and that they may have *it* more abundantly" (John 10:10).

I am a Chapter Five "poster woman." I'm not just writing about the Fifth Chapter. I'm in it with you. I want and have the "abundant life." Despite all the age-defying makeups, masques, and surgeries, sooner or later, life catches up to you. The question is, can you catch up to life? *Your life.* When my kids were young, and I had to make meals and run them to practices and sleepovers, I wondered if they'd ever grow up. Now they have. And so have I.

As the younger of my two sons, Christopher, walked across the Princeton University stage five years ago to accept his bachelor's degree, of course we celebrated him. But then I celebrated myself. I was a mom who was finally free of his tuition payments! I looked fabulous. I was fine and fit. I was a woman who, through authoring books and back-of-the-room sales of those books, speeches, preaching, and pastoring on a very low salary, and at least two side jobs, all the time, had saved enough and worked hard enough to be free enough to take a year to define how free I wanted to be and what I wanted my freedom to look like. Chris had a job that started the next day, and Sam, his older brother, was entering his third year of medical school. Without debt and without guilt, it was time to move on to the next chapter. I initially thought of doing an *Eat, Pray, Love* kind of journey and going overseas for a few months, but I've learned that I function better if I am near my sons—not on top of them, but near them. We are East Coast kind of people who always want to be within a few hours of getting to one another if and when the need arises.

In my book *Soul Sisters: Devotions for and from African American, Latina, and Asian Women,* I included a letter to my sons that said, "I have to learn how to mother and not smother." Our grown children no longer need us to hold their hands. We've trained them and taught them life lessons all along the way, and now they must be on their own journey. We cannot live it for them or allow them to stay forever dependent on us. Our job now is to be supportive of them. At this writing, I'm proud to say that my oldest, now a medical resident, just received his first paycheck—which was my signal to cancel the American Express card I had given him in my name—and my youngest, now an entrepreneur, has been financially independent, for four years, only calling to ask for advice on things like car and rental insurance.

In 2020, COVID-19 put the whole world on pause. For a few months, my older son had been back with me. I was ready to fly in my golden years. I had a great group of friends, and we were living on the waterfront, having brunch and enjoying Life 101. But COVID-19 forced the whole world to rearrange our lives, to reprioritize. For me, during the pandemic I've had precious time with the Lord and have learned to make new spiritual and physical moves towards God, towards family, and away from my food-laden cabinets.

Success to Significance

At a certain point, you must ask yourself: what does success really look like? At thirty it's one thing, and at forty it's another. But at fifty and beyond, we start looking at what mark we're making in the world, not just for ourselves, but for the generations who follow. It's called legacy. At this point, our lives shouldn't be about trying to make it to every single event or dressing to impress. Instead, our focus should be: what will my presence in this world mean? What difference will it make if I show up? As I write, this is the weekend of the Congressional Black Caucus (CBC). I hang out with various friends because I really enjoy the weekend. One of my hangout partners is forty-something. She wants to attend every single event, even if it means staying up all night long and burning the candle at both ends. I, on the other hand, hardly have any wick left in my candle after forty-plus consecutive years of attending! In her, I see a new generation or two of future leaders who I know will make a difference in this world. So, I enjoy watching them lead and spending time with them. If they want to "sit at my feet" and ask me questions, I am there for them. One just posted on Instagram how my life and ministry made a difference for so many women in ministry. That soothes my soul and tells me that there was some significance to all that I've done or tried to do. In other words, now you can sit back and thank God that God used you for all those miles in your journey where you made a difference in someone's life. No matter who you are, you did make a difference to someone you know, or even don't know.

A Toast to the Fifth-Chapter Women I Admire

Many women have been catalysts to my personal development, to my desire to do more, and to live out my Fifth Chapter on my own terms. I have been honored to connect with many of them, at different stages in my life and development, and recognize them for their fierceness is my pleasure.

Meg Armstrong: An executive coach and international consultant, Meg is invited around the world to help women leaders as they become elevated to national and international office. Whether that's in corporate America or in teaching prime ministers or presidents, she is the go-to person. Meg helped prepare me for my White House fellowship and continues to be in demand. She also has a home base, married well into her Fifth Chapter, and is living her best life. She and her husband strike the right balance between work and play.

Former First Lady Michelle Obama: After eight years in the White House, Michelle doesn't feel that she has to appear at *every* public function and chooses how she wants to spend her time. She has more than paid her dues. When she is not on tour promoting her bestseller book *Becoming* or developing the Obama Foundation for future leaders or finding content for her Netflix shows, she enjoys family and fun.

Susan Taylor: Former editor-in-chief of *Essence* magazine, she now heads the National CARES Mentoring Movement and helps youth around the nation get on the right path. Susan is an example of a woman having a successful career and then shifting gears to embark on a new mission to give back and to help future generations.

Mercedes A. Nesfield: Now in her late eighties, Mercedes exercises every week, helps with three choirs at her church, and is godmother and village mother to so many in Harlem. She has an infectious spirit that everyone wants to be around.

Her Excellencies Career Ambassador Ruth A. Davis and **Ambassador Mattie Sharpsus:** These two phenomenal women, along with the ABAA, mentor young men and women who want to enter the foreign service.

Sue Taylor, a minister who sits on the Religious Freedom Roundtable, and **Lou Ann Sabatier** of the 21Wilberforce Project, a Christian human-rights organization, who makes sure women's voices are heard globally.

Side by Side

One plus one equals two—except when two number ones stand side-by-side and equal eleven! How powerful strength in numbers really is! We saw this with the daughters of Zelophehad. You can have soul sisters who spiritually connect with you, and you can walk into this new season together. I cannot tell you how amazingly important it is for me, even on the beaches in beautiful Sag Harbor, New York, to sit and share with the women who are all in my age category. I hear stories of body changes, love interests, children, and grandchildren. When I arrive at whatever season or destination, I know I have companions who can help me along the way.

A big occurrence that happens for many in the Fifth Chapter is that we may lose a parent or other loved one. I am thankful for a group of women we call Isis from the Greek myth Isis who put the scattered pieces of men back together (not the terrorist group), after the Egyptian goddess who put the pieces of her broken husband back together again. For many in the Black community, she represents the brokenness of our men from racism. It could be our husbands, sons, or significant others.

We share our stories, side by side. In the room, there is nothing but "safe space," and we speak with confidence and with confidants. Many of us lost our mothers within a two- or three-year time period. It was the stories of the sisters who walked side by side with me that made the difference and carried me through.

Creating the Life You Want

As I reflect concluding this book to begin a new chapter in our lives, I am reminded of a book by Mel Blanchard, *A Trip to the Beach*, Three Rivers Press, 2001. In this great book, Mel talks about how he and his wife, Melinda, made a decision to create the life they wanted. It took a few years, but they had a plan. They'd been going to the islands every year. They moved from the cold Northeast to a small tropical island. They were in the restaurant business and trained the island staff to run a restaurant until they were able to do it independently. Blanchard then switched places with forty-two people on the island. They sent the islanders who they had trained to run the restaurant business, and who wanted to go, to run their restaurant in Vermont, while they ran the restaurant on the island. The Blanchards are truly living their "happily ever after."

Another book that is very significant, especially in light of the chaos and trauma that the United States has been going through, is *The Book of Joy: Lasting Happiness in a Changing World* by Douglas Abrams, the fourteenth Dalai Lama, and Archbishop Desmond Tutu. Two chapters stand out to me: "You Are a Masterpiece in the Making" and "Gratitude: I Am Fortunate to be Alive." Those chapters really sum up our lives of faith and our relationship with the Almighty God. The Dalai Lama says we need to develop "mental immunity," which is learning to avoid the destructive emotions and to develop the positive ones. That's how we get through this season and enjoy it.

Our lives are filled with rich, sad, tragic, happy, and funny stories. You don't need to add to the story; you just need to "tell it like it is," how it happened, for better, for worse, for richer, for poorer—and that, my sisters, is wisdom. I can't tell you how many offers I now have to write and film my memoirs, tell the stories of my time in government, my trailblazing in the ministry, my experience of being on the front lines of 9/11, and those wonderful childhood years as a northern child going "down South" to visit maternal relatives. Those are the life experiences and stories that only *I* can tell. Only *you* can tell your life stories. It' s not the same as when our mothers were in their fifties and making a scrapbook of news clippings and photos. Those were good for their time period, but now so many more creative tools are available to us through multimedia approaches and wonderful photography. People desire to hear your pre–Chapter Five. You can create and live the life you love and love the life you live. You can soar! Your Chapter Five says, "I'm ready to handle life and have it more abundantly!"

> *"God is the God of 'right now.' He doesn't want you sitting around regretting yesterday. Nor does He want you wringing your hands and worrying about the future. He wants you focusing on what He is saying to you and putting in front of you ... right now."*—Priscilla Shirer[23]

Thank you, God, that I won't die wondering, "What if I tried?" I'm getting up, right now, and going for it.

Ready or not, here I come! Although this book ends, your fabulous next Chapter Five begins!

A Letter to My Younger Self

"I'd tell my 20-year-old self, 'Don't be afraid to do it all. Whatever you're interested in, just go for it. Don't wait around for a better time.'"
—Angela Bassett[24]

This quote by the incredibly talented, beautiful, award-winning Fifth Chapter actress Angela Bassett (and my Centennial Line Soror of Delta Sigma Theta) made me think about the transference of knowledge and wisdom that we can share with the younger generation of women today. What would your letter to your twenty-year-old self look like? Start writing yours today and share it with your Fifth Chapter sisters on DrSujay.Live. Here's mine:

Dear Suzan with a "z,"

Before you were "Sujay," before you were
Rev. Dr. Ambassador, you were just Suzan,
non-pretentious, non-competitive. You were
a girl with dreams, big dreams, a big God, and
a wonderful family and extended family, who
always loved and embraced you. You never
lacked for anything, not only materially, but
you had guts, "gumption," as they say down
South, and you were never afraid to ask for
what you wanted.
   You loved being happy and seeing everyone in
the room smile. Make a point to always find
people and places that allow you to know
it's your turn to smile for yourself and be
in rooms with people who help to keep that
smile on your face. You're from Harlem and
the Boogie Down Bronx, so dancing is in your
bones. Never lose your joy. Keep dancing. Keep
smiling. Rainy days will come, and when they
do, sometimes you have to bring your sun-
shine with you. You were born to shine even
in the darkest places. Try not to let your
light go out, for your light comes from God.
Jesus is your light, so don't try to hide it.
Use everything God gave you. "This little light
of mine, I'm gonna let it shine. Let it shine,
let it shine, let it shine." Let the "son" shine.

As you are learning to drive, some days it may seem like it's darker and difficult to see the road ahead. But know that you get 30 feet of light. Keep driving and you'll get another 30 feet until you reach your destination. Sometimes it may seem difficult to merge onto the highway and you are stuck at the "on" ramp as the traffic keeps coming, and it's coming fast. Don't lose heart, as there's always a "break" in traffic. Although you may have to wait a few minutes, stay focused, as your break will surely come.

The ironic thing is that life's highway is the same way. Do not rush your life and desire to be so grown. Wait for your turn, and then seize it, squeeze it, and enjoy the ride. Just choose one lane at a time, stay in your lane, and you will arrive safely at your destination. Try to avoid the detours and dead ends that your parents and other adults warned you about. But should they come, there's always a way to get back on the right road. You can't reverse, but you can shift gears to neutral and idle until you find your path. You can make a "You" turn and then go straight ahead. Forward is the only way to go.

Life is yours for the taking. You can have it all, but not all at once. Take life in doses;

swallowing, tasting, savoring life's wonderful moments, and stopping long enough to see and smell the roses. You don't have to go fast, yet you can cruise at the speed limit and go far. When you feel like you're running out of steam, just stop. Put your gear in park and assess where you are and how far you have to go. God rested. And if God can rest, so can you.

Remember these two words that will take you farther than you ever imagined: "thank you." Folks don't have to be nice to you, so when they are, show them your appreciation. Enjoy every day and every season of life. Work hard, pay your dues, and play hard. There will be salty, there will be sour, and there will be sweet, but all flavors will bring about their own lesson and growth. Sometimes oil has to mix with water, and if shaken, they become one. You are blessed, my child. Now live like it. Act like it. Love like it. Your best days are ahead. Hang in there and be fabulous!

Your Next Move: A Letter to My Younger Self

Write a letter to your younger self.

Covenant with Myself

I, _____ (insert your name and say it OUT LOUD), promise to give myself permission to have joy, happiness, and fulfillment, and to be absolutely fabulous. I will not go back, turn back, or put myself down. I will merge onto the highway of life, choose the lane I want to be in today, go forward.

> *I'm pressing on the upward way,*
> *New heights I'm gaining every day;*
> *Still praying as I onward bound,*
> *"Lord, plant my feet on higher*
> *ground."* —Johnson Oatman, Jr.[25]

Repeat as often as you want to, and as often as necessary!

Endnotes

1. Jen Sincero, *You Are a Badass: How to Stop Doubting Your Greatness and Start Living an Awesome Life* (Philadelphia: Running Press, 2013).

2. Although this quote is often credited to advice columnist Ann Landers, its origin remains unknown. See https://www.politifact.com/factchecks/2019/oct/25/viral-image/no-evidence-ann-landers-said-quote-about-age/.

3. Gary Chapman, *The 5 Love Languages* (Chicago: Northfield Publishing, 2015).

4. See https://www.goodreads.com/quotes/724216-today-is-the-oldest-you-ve-ever-been-and-the-youngest.

5. See https://www.thecut.com/2021/03/25-famous-women-on-aging.html.

6. Stephen R. Covey, *The 7 Habits of Highly Effective People: Powerful Lessons on Personal Change* (New York: Simon & Shuster, 2013).

7. Matthew Street, "What does the number five mean in the Bible?", BibleReflections.net, bible-reflections.net/resource/what-does-the-number-five-mean-the-bible/2848, accessed January 20, 2021.

8. See http://inaword.org/thank_god_i_am_not_a_woman.html.

9. Abarim Publications, http://www.abarim-publications.com/Meaning/Mahlah.html#.XbTJaujYo3F.

10. Abarim Publications, http://www.abarim-publications.com/Meaning/Noah.html#.XbTJ6ejYo3G.

11. Abarim Publications, http://www.abarim-publications.com/Meaning/Milcah.html#.XbTIY-jYo3E.

12. Abarim Publications, http://www.abarim-publications.com/Meaning/Tirzah.html#.XbTLDOjYo3E.

13. Abarim Publications, https://www.abarim-publications.com/Meaning/Hoglah.html.

14. M.G. Easton M.A., D.D., *Illustrated Bible Dictionary*, Third Edition, published by Thomas Nelson, 1897, Public Domain, https://www.biblestudytools.com/dictionary/partridge/.

15. Martin Luther King Jr., *Strength to Love* (Minneapolis: Fortress Press, 2010).

16. Coretta Scott King and Barbara Reynolds, *My Life, My Love, My Legacy: The Life of Coretta Scott King* (New York: Henry Holt and Company, 2017).

17. George Bernard Shaw, *Annajanska, the Bolsevik Empress,* a one-act play first performed at the London Coliseum, January 21, 1918.

18. This quote is often attributed to C. S. Lewis, but there is no evidence that it originated with him.

19. Julie Kosin, "Glenn Close Gives Emotional, Rousing Golden Globes Acceptance Speech," Harper's Bazaar, January 6, 2019, https://www.harpersbazaar.com/culture/film-tv/a25770458/glenn-close-golden-globes-acceptance-speech/.

20. Michelle Obama, keynote address at the Young African Women Leaders Forum, Regina Mundi Church, in Soweto, South Africa, June 22, 2011.

21. Suze Orman, *Women & Money: Be Strong, Be Smart, Be Secure* (New York: Random House, 2018).

22. Gwendolyn Goldsby Grant, *Essence*—Speech at women's breakfast

23. From a sermon preached by Priscilla Shirer at First Baptist Church of Glenarden, MD, 2019.

24. Angela Bassett, https//www.brainyquote.com/quotes/angela_bassett_909104.

25. Johnson Oatman, Jr., "I'm Pressing on the Upward Way." https://hymnary.org/text/im_pressing_on_the_upward_way, public domain.

Selected Bibliography

1. Anderson, Jane. *The Wife*. Film directed by Björn L. Runge. Based on the novel *The Wife* by Meg Wolitzer. New York: Scribner, 2004.

2. Covey, Stephen R. *The 7 Habits of Highly Effective People: Powerful Lessons on Personal Change*. New York: Simon & Shuster, 2013.

3. King, Martin Luther Jr. *Strength to Love*. Minneapolis: Fortress Press, 2010.

4. King, Coretta Scott, and Barbara Reynolds, *My Life, My Love, My Legacy: The Life of Coretta Scott King*. New York: Henry Holt and Company, 2017.

5. Orman, Suze. *Women & Money: Be Strong, Be Smart, Be Secure*. New York: Random House, 2018.

6. Sincero, Jen. *You Are a Badass: How to Stop Doubting Your Greatness and Start Living an Awesome Life*. Philadelphia: Running Press, 2013.

Recommended Reading

Blanchard, Robert and Melinda Blanchard. *Live What You Love: Notes from an Unusual Life*. New York: Sterling, 2005.

Blanchard, Bob and Melinda Blanchard. *Changing Your Course: The 5-Step Guide to Getting the Life You Want*. New York: Sterling, 2008.

Cook, Suzan Johnson. *Balancing Your Life: God's Plan for Hope and A Future*. Nashville: Thomas Nelson, 2006.

Cook, Suzan Johnson. *Becoming a Woman of Destiny: Turning Life's Trials into Triumphs!* New York: Tarcher-Perigee, 2010.

Cook, Suzan Johnson. *Sister's Guide to Survive and Thrive in Ministry, The*. Valley Forge: Judson Press, 2019.

Cook, Suzan Johnson. *Soul Sisters: Devotions for and from African American, Asian and Latina Women*. New York: TarcherPerigee, 2016.

Cook, Suzan Johnson, and Susan Denise Cook, ed. *Sister to Sister: Devotions for and from African American Women*. Valley Forge: Judson Press, 1995.

Cook, Suzan Johnson. *Too Blessed to be Stressed: Words of Wisdom for Women on the Move*. Nashville: Thomas Nelson, Inc., 1998.

Crandell, Susan. *Thinking about Tomorrow: Reinventing Yourself at Midlife*. (New York: Grand Central Life & Style, 2007.

Crawford, Caretha. *Determined to Succeed: Power Principles to Get What's Yours*. Maitland, FL: Xulon Press, 2016.

Dalai Lama, Desmond Tutu, and Douglas Carlton Abrams. *The Book of Joy: Lasting Happiness in a Changing World*. New Orleans: Cornerstone Book Publishers, 2016.

Kimbro, Dennis P. *What Makes The Great Great: Strategies for Extraordinary Achievement*. New York: Crown Publishing Group, 1998.

King, Coretta Scott, and Barbara Reynolds. *My Life, My Love, My Legacy: The Life of Coretta Scott King*. New York: Henry Holt and Company, 2017.

McKeithen, Sheila R. *Twelve Steps to Your Healing*. San Francisco: HarperOne, 1992.

Meyer, Joyce. *The Confident Woman: Start Today Living Boldly and Without Fear*. Nashville: FaithWords, 2010.

Ponder, Catherine. *The Millionaire from Nazareth: His Prosperity Secrets for You!* Camarillo, CA: Devorss & Company, 1979.

Rushnell, Squire. *When God Winks: How the Power of Coincidence Guides Your Life*. New York: Howard Books, 2018.

Strahan, Michael. "From Defensive Tackle to Lifestyle Guru," *Delta Sky*, February 2019.

St. James, Elaine. *Simplify Your Life: 100 Ways to Slow Down and Enjoy the Things That Really Matter*. New York: Hachette Books, 1994.

Taylor, Barbara Brown. *Leaving Church: A Memoir of Faith*. New York: HarperOne, 2009.

Tutu, Desmond. *God Has a Dream: A Vision of Hope for Our Time*. New York: Image, 2005.

Underwood, Jim. *More than a Pink Cadillac: Mary Kay's Inc.'s 9 Leadership Keys to Success*. New York: McGrawHill, 2002.

About the Author
Rev. Dr. Ambassador Suzan Johnson Cook
(Ambassador Sujay, Dr. Sujay, and "Dr. Fabulous")

She brings the world together through business, education, diplomacy, and faith

A faith leader, entrepreneur, educator, success strategist, international influencer, communications expert, and diplomat, Suzan Johnson Cook was the first female and African American to hold the position of U.S. Ambassador for International Religious Freedom. Nominated by Secretary of State Hillary Clinton and appointed by President Barack Obama, she was the principal advisor to the President of the United States and Secretary of State, for religious freedom, globally, having all 199 countries in her portfolio, and integrating religious freedom into the foreign policy and national security discussions. She represented the United States in twenty-eight countries and more than one hundred diplomatic engagements, bringing faith leaders and women to the Religious Freedom table. Additionally, she has been the faith advisor to two U.S. presidents, three cabinet secretaries, as well as political and celebrity leaders. She served as President Bill Clinton's only faith advisor on the historic "President's Initiative on Race." On the front lines of 9/11, she helped New York and our nation through traumatic times and became known as "America's Chaplain." In 2016, she was the only woman to run for New York City's thirteenth congressional district. She was made an honorary member of Delta Sigma Theta Sorority, Inc., in its centennial year, and is a proud soror of the Centennial 6 Line.

Currently she serves as CEO and founder of the Global Black Women's Chamber of Commerce, the first chamber solely dedicated to Black Women business owners. Recently, she received a one-million-dollar grant from the Lilly Endowment, the R.E.A.L. Black Women In Ministry THRIVE initiative to help Black women to advance and be placed in parish ministries.

She has expertise and experience in higher education, domestic and foreign policy, called upon often to be a media commentator, guest lecturer, Visiting Fellow, and panel moderator. She served Harvard's Divinity School as an Associate Dean, and faculty member for three years, as a President's Administrative Fellow. Her alma mater, Union Theological Seminary, awarded her with the UNITAS and Trailblazing awards, as well as the Activist Scholar Fellowship for two years. She also was a Fellow at Catholic University of America, where she concentrated on women and peacebuilding.

Ambassador "Sujay" (a nickname for "Suzan J") held the rank of Inspector, as Chaplain to the New York City Police Department for twenty-one years, the first woman to serve in that role. She helped to bridge relations between the NYPD and New York's diverse communities. She was also the first and only female president of the historic Hampton University Ministers Conference, the largest gathering of African American clergy in the world, in its 102-year history. She served as pastor for three NYC congregations, including the famous standing-room-only "Lunch Hour of Power," mid-week services and seminars for the business community. Her film, *A Different Way,* which describes her work at 9/11 and with religious freedom, won first place in the "Dare to Overcome" film festival, awarded in Tokyo, Japan, in 2019 and was accepted into the Cannes Film Festival 2021, in the Afrique Pavillion.

Her passion is education, and she desires to shape a generation of twenty-first-century scholars and to enhance the role that women play as leaders, both domestically and internationally. Her WOW and Pro-Voice/Pro Voz Movements are in direct response to seeing firsthand the lack of access, and the lack of women at corporate, political, and diplomatic tables worldwide. Sheryl Sandberg says "Lean in." Ambassador Sujay says, "We've got to 'get in.'" Domestically, her movement helps Black, Latina, and Asian women become both a political and economic force through connections, celebrations, and conversations, mentoring them into key leadership positions, providing life balance, and launching retreats to help them soar in their chosen professions and vocations in mind, body, and spirit.

Recently she served as Distinguished Visiting Professor of the Religious Freedom Center's LUCE Foundations' Intensive for Historically Black Theological Institutions.

Owner of Charisma Speakers, the only global professional speakers bureau owned by a Black woman, and a full cross-cultural communications firm, she serves as an agent for and provides keynote speakers, training, and global experts around the world, for corporations, colleges/universities, conventions, and conferences. She has given more than three thousand speeches.

A civil, gender, and human-rights activist, she officiated the Celebration of Life services for her mentor and godmother, civil-rights legend Coretta Scott King. She has addressed the United Nations, the U.N. General Assembly, and U.N. Geneva. A frequent contributor to CNN, MSNBC, FOX, BBC TV, and other major media, she also writes a column for *Huffington Post*, Thrive Global, and has authored fifteen books. She is the mother of two adult sons and lives in both Washington, DC, and New York.

Ambassador Suzan Johnson Cook is highly regarded as one who bridges party, racial, and gender divides. She can be reached at CharismaSpeakers@gmail.com or GlobalBlackWomenCC@gmail.com.

Or connect with her on social media via LinkedIn.com/in/AmbassadorSujay or Facebook.com/SujayJohnson.